man
and his
environment:
food

man
and his
environment
series:

edited by
John Bardach
(*The University of Hawaii*)
Marston Bates
and Stanley Cain
(*The University of Michigan*)

WASTE: by Wesley Marx

LAW: by Earl Finbar Murphy,
The Ohio State University

CLIMATE: by David M. Gates,
The University of Michigan

FOOD: by Lester R. Brown,
Overseas Development Council,
and Gail W. Finsterbusch,
The Urban Institute

man
and his
environment:
food

LESTER R. BROWN
Overseas Development Council
and
GAIL W. FINSTERBUSCH
The Urban Institute

'87

Harper & Row, Publishers
New York
Evanston
San Francisco
London

man
and his
environment:
food

Standard Book Number:
06-040983-5 (Paperback Edition)
06-040984-3 (Clothbound Edition)

Library of Congress Catalog Card
Number: 76-178104

Cover photo:
Georg Gerster, Rapho Guillumette

contents

editors' introduction

The books of the Harper & Row series being published under the general title of *Man and His Environment* are designed to help us understand the world about us, our dependence on it, and what we are doing to it, both good and bad.

From the personal point of view, the environment is "everything else but me." It is the sky over our heads and the earth beneath our feet. It is other people and any living animal or plant with which we have any connections. It includes what the senses of sight, hearing, taste, smell, and touch tell us about nature. Also, the environment is home, the cities and towns we have built. It includes the landscape that is altered by raising food, feed, and fiber; by the extraction of minerals; by building homes, schools, churches, places of business, and factories; and by building facilities for travel and transport, for the generation of energy, and for communication. The environment includes not only the natural and man-made things about us but also physical and cultural conditions and processes.

All these elements of the environment can be studied, thought about, and worked with individually, but this analytic approach is inadequate for the understanding of the total environment, and it leads to difficulties when we overlook or neglect the consequences of single-purpose actions. This is because the elements of the environment do not occur singly in nature or in culture, but in complex interacting systems. For example, soil is not just decomposed rock. It includes air and water, hundreds of organic and inorganic compounds, and almost innumerable living things, most of which are too small to be seen in a handful of dirt. Water is a simple compound, but we are not likely to encounter it as such. Many substances are dissolved in it, particles are suspended in it, and living creatures float and swim about in it. Everywhere we find mixtures of things, in a drop of pond water, a lump of soil, a breath of air, most things that man makes. Not only do we find mixtures of things everywhere; these things interact with one another because of processes of their own, changing one another and the conditions of the whole.

In this book of the series Lester R. Brown and Gail W. Finsterbusch have dealt with one important facet of the interrelations between man and his environment. For each of these books, no matter what is the main focus (climate, energy, materials, waste, food, population, recreation, transportation, law, or aesthetics and the cultural roots of our viewpoints), we have asked the authors to take a holistic point of view and to write about interconnections, interactions, consequences, and, in fact, the systems of man and nature together. As broadgauged thinkers and scientists, they are well equipped for this demanding goal.

Man has become the leading cause of environmental change. He is discovering his own responsibility for much that he does not like—air and water pollution, poisons in his food, deteriorated cities—and that in order to correct such disagreeable, unhealthy, and unpleasant conditions he must understand his own ecology.

Although this book can stand alone, it is also an integral part of the series on *Man and His Environment*.

John E. Bardach
Marston Bates
Stanley A. Cain

preface

Thomas Malthus was probably the first to detect worldwide population pressure and to identify world population growth as a problem. When he published his essay on *The Principle of Population* in 1798, he defined the population problem primarily in terms of food supplies and the threat of famine. For almost 200 years men have perceived the population–food problem in these terms, asking "Can we produce enough food to feed anticipated human numbers?"

In man's quest for more and more food to meet mounting needs in modern times, he has rapidly extended and intensified agricultural intervention in the earth's ecosystem. Food production has kept pace with population growth, but with disturbing ecological consequences. The relevant question is no longer "Can we produce enough food?" but "What are the environmental consequences of attempting to do so?"

Adverse environmental consequences associated with continually expanding the production of food are already serious and certain to become much worse. They are increasing in number and severity. Sharpening awareness of them may well cause man to depart from the present

demographic path, and to lower birth rates through decisions taken on the individual, national, and global levels.

Lester R. Brown
Gail W. Finsterbusch

man
and his
environment:
food

1
history, geography, and economics of malnutrition

Man's existence in relation to his food supply has always been precarious. For pre-agricultural man, the risk lay mainly in the uncertainty of the hunt, an uncertainty faced for hundreds of thousands of years. Although he has overcome the uncertainty of the hunt, agricultural man has perennially faced the possibility of crop failure due to the vicissitudes of weather or other natural causes.

It is true that the earth's food-producing capacity and man's food supply have expanded enormously since the invention of agriculture. But the size of the human population has always tended to press against the limits of the food supply regardless of its magnitude. This has resulted in chronic or at least seasonal hunger for most of mankind throughout most of its existence. In the past, this tendency has also resulted in the deaths of large numbers of people when sudden, sharp, catastrophic reductions in food supply, due most often to natural disasters but sometimes to man-made causes such as civil disorder and war, have occurred periodically.

Whether it results from natural or man-made causes, severe famine is always a horror. Not only do humans suffer and die in large numbers, but many are pressed to extreme behavior under the duress of starvation. Besides hoarding and stealing food, starving people have been known to eat vermin, clay, and pulverized bones; to sell children to obtain money for food; and to resort to suicide, murder, and cannibalism. Rather than slowly starve to death, thousands of Romans allegedly threw themselves into the Tiber during a famine in 436 B.C. And whole families are reported to have drowned themselves in the Indian famine of A.D. 1291. Chroniclers mention cannibalism occurring in pretwentieth-century famines in England, Scotland, Ireland, Italy, Egypt, India, and in China in at least fifteen famines. Cannibalism is linked with famine in the twentieth century as well—for example, in Russia, in 1921 and 1933. Cemeteries in many parts of Russia had to be guarded from 1921 to 1922 in order to prevent exhumation of freshly buried corpses.

Asiatic famines are in a class by themselves in terms of frequency and mortality. Asia's rice-growing areas, supporting the earth's largest and densest populations, have been particularly susceptible. Much of Asia lies within the monsoon belt, where rainfall is unreliable—sometimes failing altogether, sometimes coming in excess. Modern Asia, containing more than half the world's people, continues to be the part of the planet most vulnerable to massive famine due to natural catastrophe.

India and China are the sites of the worst known historical famines. In India more than 10 million people, perhaps as much as a fifth of the population and a number equal to man the hunter's total global population, perished in the drought-caused Bengal famine of 1769–1770. Cornelius Walford, in the earliest serious effort to compile a worldwide chronology of famines, included the following description of this Indian famine:

> . . . *The air was so infected by the noxious effluvia of dead
> bodies, that it was scarcely possible to stir abroad without
> perceiving it; and without hearing also the frantic cries
> of the victims of famine who were seen at every stage of
> suffering and death. Whole families expired, and villages*

were desolated. When the new crop came forward in August it had in many cases no owners. *

During the Indian famine of 1866, over 1 million persons starved to death. Another 1.5 million died in Rajputana in 1869; 5 million from 1876 to 1878; and 1 million more in 1900.

In China, between 9 and 13 million perished in a famine lasting from 1877 to 1879. The *Times* (London) carried a telegram on March 13, 1878, reporting famine conditions and appealing for aid:

Appalling famine raging throughout four provinces North China. Nine million people reported destitute. Children daily sold in markets for [raising means to procure] food. Foreign Relief Committees appeal to England and America for assistance. †

An interview with an eyewitness from Shanghai, which was included in the same newspaper, revealed that people's faces were black with hunger; that they were dying thousands upon thousands; that women, girls, and boys were openly offered for sale to any chance wayfarer; and that parents were known to kill their children when it was impossible to dispose of them rather than witness their prolonged sufferings, and then often committed suicide by arsenic or by throwing themselves down wells. It has been estimated that during the early decades of the twentieth century in China, deaths by starvation reached into the tens of thousands most years in some parts of the country and probably averaged more than a million per decade.

Africa, too, has suffered from famine, although not with the same cost of life as in Asiatic famines. Much of East Africa also lies within the monsoon belt and is subject to weather variations similar to those that trouble Asia. An in-

*Cornelius Walford, *Famines of the World: Past and Present* (London: Edward Stanford, 1879), p. 12.

†*London Times*, as quoted in *Ibid*., p. 18.

credibly severe and tenacious famine struck Egypt in North Africa in the eleventh century when the Nile floods failed seven years in a row. Walford gives the following description of this famine:

For seven successive years the overflow of the Nile failed, and with it almost the entire subsistence of the country, while the rebels interrupted supplies of grain from the north. Two provinces were entirely depopulated; in another half the inhabitants perished; while in Cairo City (El-Kahvich) the people were reduced to the direst straits. Bread was sold for 14 dirhems to the loaf; and all provisions being exhausted, the worst horrors of famine followed. The wretched resorted to cannibalism, and organized bands kidnapped the unwary passenger in the desolate streets, principally by means of ropes furnished with hooks and let down from the latticed windows. In the year 1072 the famine reached its height. It was followed by a pestilence, and this again was succeeded by an invading army. *

West Africa, although it has experienced chronic minor food shortages, has no record of catastrophic famine due to natural causes; and there were none due to man-made causes prior to Biafra.

Europe experienced numerous historical famines resulting from both natural and man-made causes. The European continent may have claim to a higher incidence of severe man-made famines than any other region of the world. Ireland, plagued by recurrent famine due to war and civil disruption, adopted the potato as a food staple in an effort to protect its food supply against recurrent burning and destruction by the English. Ironically, the Irish potato famine is the classic example of massive famine resulting from the destruction of the food crop by plant disease. When the potato crop was struck by blight in 1846, Ireland's population was around 8 million.

* *Ibid.*, p. 7.

The famine of 1846–1847 killed about 1.5 million people. Large-scale emigration to the United States followed in the ensuing decades. Famine together with the delayed marriages and low birth rates over the century and a quarter since the famine have reduced Ireland's population to 4 million—just half of what it was when the potato blight hit.

Whereas Western Europe endured many famines in the past, particularly in medieval times, during recent centuries improved communication and transportation have increasingly facilitated the movement of food to food-deficit and famine-threatened areas. Acute food shortages in modern times have resulted from war and have been confined to small local areas such as Vienna in 1919 or the Warsaw ghetto in 1942. They have not resulted in high mortality. Eastern Europe, however, has experienced two massive famines in the twentieth century, both in Russia: one, in 1920–21, was caused by drought; and another, in 1932–1933, resulted from large-scale social displacement and reorganization during the collectivization period. The Soviet famine of the 1930s, in which an estimated 3 to 10 million died, was the last major European famine. The Netherlands was on the brink of famine toward the end of, and right after, World War II, with many Dutch close to death. But high mortality was averted.

North America has never experienced major famine, largely because of relatively dependable rainfall, the absence of major wars, and an overall favorable balance between population and food-producing resources. In fact, North America has shipped an increasing proportion of the food produced on its land abroad, particularly following the United States Civil War, and literally became the breadbasket of the world after World War II. With one exception, Latin America, too, has been remarkably free of massive famine. One catastrophic famine occurred among the Toltecs in Mexico in the eleventh century, resulting in large migration and probably the origination of human sacrifice.

An actual list of the known massive historical famines is surprisingly short, totaling 36. Compiling such a list is difficult because data are scanty and questionable. In 1963, Geoffrey

table 1
reasonably authenticated major famines

date	place	comments
B.C.		
436	Rome	Thousands of starving people threw themselves into the Tiber
A.D.		
310	England	40,000 deaths
917-918	India (Kashmir)	Great mortality
c. 1051	Mexico	Caused migration of Toltecs; probable origin of human sacrifice
1064-1072	Egypt	Failure of Nile flood for 7 years; cannibalism reported
1069	England	Harrying by Normans; cannibalism
1344-1345	India	Many thousands of deaths
1347	Italy	Famine followed by plague (the "Black Death") caused great mortality
1594-1598	Asia	In India, great mortality, cannibalism, and bodies not disposed of
1600	Russia	500,000 deaths from famine and plague
1630	India (Deccan)	30,000 deaths in Surat alone
1660-1661	India	No rain for 2 years
1677	India (Hyderabad)	Due to excessive rain; great mortality
1769	France	5 percent of population said to have died
1769-1770	India (Bengal)	Due to drought; 10 million deaths
1770	Eastern Europe	Famine and disease caused 168,000 deaths in Bohemia, 20,000 in Russia and Poland
1775	Cape Verde Islands	16,000 deaths
1790-1792	India (Bombay, Hyderabad)	*Doji Bara*, or skull famine; bodies not disposed of; great mortality
1803-1804	Western India	Due to drought, locusts, and war; thousands died
1837-1838	Northwestern India	800,000 deaths
1846-1847	Ireland	Due to potato blight; 2-3 million deaths

table 1 (Continued)

date	place	comments
1866	India (Bengal, Orissa)	1 million deaths
1869	India (Rajputana)	1.5 million deaths
1874–1875	Asia Minor	150,000 deaths
1876–1878	India	5 million deaths
1876–1879	Northern China	Almost no rain for 3 years; deaths estimated at 9–13 million
1891–1892	Russia	Widespread distress; mortality relatively small
1899–1900	India	1 million deaths
1918–1919	Uganda	4,400 deaths
1920–1921	Northern China	500,000 deaths
1920–1921	Russia	Due to drought; millions died
1929	China (Hunan)	2 million deaths
1932–1933	Russia	Due to collectivization; excess mortality estimated at 3–10 million
1943	Ruanda-Urandi	35,000–50,000 deaths
1943–1944	India (Bengal)	Excessive rain and wartime difficulty of supply; 2–4 million deaths
1969–1970	Biafra	Due to civil war; several hundred thousand deaths (minimum)

Bussell Masefield published the most satisfactory compilation to date, and the list of major famines in Table 1 is adapted from his study. Only three of the famines listed are clearly man – made: the English famine of 1069, the Soviet famine of 1932–1933, and the Biafran famine of 1969–1970. Up to the present, most massive famines have been caused by the vagaries of weather.

The last great famine due to the vicissitudes of weather occurred in West Bengal in 1943 when flooding destroyed the rice crop, costing some 2 to 4 million lives. Relief measures were not introduced until several weeks after the famine had begun because of the difficulty of wartime supply and communication.

Largely as a result of U.S. initiative, the world has been spared from massive famine due to natural causes in recent decades, despite the explosive growth of population in the poor countries. At the end of World War II, the United States assumed a global postwar relief role that included providing large quantities of food for Western Europe and Japan. Through this effort, the United States decided it had the agricultural technology and the food-production capacity to assume a global famine-relief role on a continuing basis, a role that became institutionalized in 1954 with the passage of Public Law 480. This legislation permits the sale of U.S. surplus foodstuffs to poor countries for payment in local currencies rather than in dollars or gold.

The U.S. food-aid program expanded rapidly following the passage of PL 480, reaching and leveling off at $1.5 billion in the 1960s. During the sixties, an average of 15 million tons of grain per year (mainly wheat) was shipped abroad under PL 480, feeding roughly 100 million people. Sending food aid to other countries both relieved food shortages abroad and reduced American food surpluses to more acceptable reserve levels.

The famine-relief policy was followed even in the mid-1960s when massive food needs developed in India after U.S. surpluses had been eliminated. It became necessary to bring idled cropland back into production for food-aid purposes. In fact, American wheat-acreage allotments were increased in 1966 by Secretary of Agriculture Orville Freeman in the face of strong domestic opposition. As it turned out, one-fifth (7 million tons) of the U.S. wheat crop was required to stave off famine in India in 1966 and again in 1967, when the monsoons failed for two consecutive years. Sixty million Indians were fed for two years entirely by food shipments from the United States. Had the United States not been able to respond, the world would have witnessed a famine resulting in the deaths of millions and possibly tens of millions, a human tragedy that would have rivaled the carnage of World War II and earlier Asiatic famines.

For the next several years, the chances of large-scale famine due to natural disaster (such as drought, flood, windstorm, crop disease, or pests) and resulting in catastrophic loss of life in a particular geographic area seem slight. Since World War II, the global production and distribution system both among and within countries has evolved to the point where large quantities of food can be moved from one country to another on a scale sufficient to avoid any natural catastrophe that can be readily envisaged. The huge quantity of food transported to India to avert famine, for example, required some 600 ships, the largest maritime assemblage since the Allied forces crossed the English Channel on D-Day. Sizable world reserves of wheat and a record surplus of rice, plus sizable acreages of idle cropland in North America, provide a buffer against massive famine for at least the next few years. Massive famine, when it does occur, will most likely be primarily man made, a result of civil disorder and war, as it was in Biafra. And the famine in beleagured Biafra could have been prevented if the world community had refused to allow the war to be settled on the basis of hunger and starvation.

Throughout man's life on earth, most of the human race has been hungry at least seasonally if not in a chronic sense—a fact of the human condition often forgotten in the well-fed, wealthier countries. Only in the course of the last 200 years, since the Industrial Revolution, has an adequate diet come to be assured to most of that third of mankind living in the rich countries of North America, Western Europe, Eastern Europe, Japan, and Australia. Except for comparatively small portions of the populations on marginal incomes, the people of these countries have a more than adequate diet, and many, in fact, are overfed. Never before has as large a portion of mankind been as well fed and secure in relation to the food supply. For the remaining two-thirds of mankind, those living in the poor countries of Asia, South America, and Africa, the ancient, ever-present threat of massive and outright famine has been lifted—for the more immediate future at least.

Nevertheless, human nutrition on a global scale is still in a sorry state. The majority of mankind is not well nourished, either in the quantity or quality of its diet. True, substantial possibilities for improvement exist; they will be discussed throughout this book. These, together with other activities of man, do, however, carry with them seeds of far-reaching ecological disturbances. Those disturbances, in relation to the problem of curbing man's numbers, will, suitably, be discussed in the final chapters of this book.

Man's food-energy or calorie requirements vary with physique, with climate, with level of physical activity. Even to sit still and just remain alive requires food energy, a minimum of 1700 calories daily for the average adult. Calorie standards for an adequate daily diet range from an average 2300 calories per capita for southern Asian countries (e.g., India, Burma, Afghanistan) to 2700 per capita for Canada and the Soviet Union. Actual consumption ranges from a low of just under 1800 calories per capita in Haiti to a high of just over 3400 per capita in Ireland and New Zealand. Most of the rich countries of North America, northern and eastern Europe, parts of South America, and Oceania consume between 3000 and 3300 calories per person daily. The result is that many of their residents suffer from overnutrition, a modern problem of growing proportions.

Perhaps the most careful and objective assessment of the global incidence of hunger is found in the United States Department of Agriculture's *World Food Budget* (Figure 1). That

figure 1. *Calorie-protein–deficient areas. (From Economic Research Service, U.S. Department of Agriculture. 1965.* The World Food Budget 1970. *Foreign Agricultural Economic Report No. 19.)*

analysis divides the world into diet-adequate countries and diet-inadequate countries on the basis of recommended minimum calorie, protein, and fat intake. In 1960, an estimated 1.9 billion people lived in countries where the average calorie intake (the main indicator of diet quantity) was below the recommended minimum. The daily food-energy deficit averaged 300 calories per person. For some countries, and for many groups and countless individuals, the gap was far wider. In southern India, for example, food-energy intake is around 1600 calories daily. Of course, many individuals receive far less than the average intake.

The hungriest nations, those having the largest calorie deficiencies, are the countries of Central America and communist Asia. The hungriest continent in terms of sheer numbers of people without enough food is Asia, where one-half of mankind resides and where all countries except Japan, Israel, Turkey, Lebanon, Malaya, and Taiwan have inadequate calorie supplies. Within some countries classified as diet-adequate on the basis of national average, there are substantial geographical regions that are poorly fed. Brazil, for example, has an average national diet that meets minimum nutritional standards. Yet the 30 million people in the cassava-eating region of the northeast do not have adequate diets. Although there was little change in diets between 1960, when the *Food Budget* calculations were made, and 1967, preliminary information suggests modest improvements in several poor countries since 1968.

Calorie intake, although a good quantitative indicator of diet adequacy, is not a good indicator of quality. Protein intake is the key indicator of diet quality in today's world. Most people suffering from calorie shortages suffer also from protein malnutrition. Protein is burned as food energy in the absence of sufficient calories from carbohydrates, sugar, and fats. But protein malnutrition is more widespread than calorie malnutrition because there are areas of the earth and segments of society where starchy staples supply sufficient calories although protein supplies are inadequate. The problem is not just a lack of protein per se (60 grams per day including at least 10 grams of animal protein is the recommended standard), but also a lack of protein of high quality such as that found in animal products or legumes (peas, beans, soybeans). Cereals contain not only much less protein than legumes, meats, and dairy foods but proteins of lesser quality.

Vitamins and minerals are other quality components that are deficient in poor diets. It is estimated that in India vitamin A deficiencies are largely responsible for the blindness of 4 million people and the partial blindness of possibly three times as many. In the same country, iron-deficiency anemia is considered responsible for 30 to 40 percent of the deaths of women in childbirth. Nutritionists emphasize protein as the major quality component, not, however, because the effects of other deficiencies are less serious, but because deficiencies in vitamins and other minerals are easier to remedy. They are required in small amounts and can be manufactured relatively cheaply.

The group for whom protein malnutrition is most serious is children between the ages of one and six. But pregnant women and nursing mothers are groups currently receiving serious nutrition research attention, particularly because of the effects their protein deficiencies may have on fetuses and nursing infants. Most children in the poor countries suffer from protein malnutrition at one time or another. Even children who received adequate protein while being breast-fed often experience protein deficiencies after weaning because of what can be called the *starchy-food phenomenon:* the transfer to a diet of easily digestible, cheap, starchy foods like cassava, cereals, and bananas. Advanced symptoms of protein malnutrition are well known: swollen bodies, peeling skin, reddish-brown, brittle hair. What is less immediately visible is the enormous toll protein malnutrition exacts on the physical and mental development of the young.

The effects of nutrition on physical development can be seen on the streets of Tokyo today. Young Japanese, well nourished from infancy as a result of the enormous rise in income and in proper nutrition in Japan since the 1940s, are noticeably taller than their elders. Some, including Japanese nutritionist Shinkichi Nagamini, speculate that Japanese may surpass Americans in physical measurements in the not-so-distant future. Coats of armor and costumes worn in the Middle Ages and the Renaissance provide evidence that, on the average, medieval and Renaissance Europeans were much smaller in stature than contemporary Europeans and Americans are. Improvement in nutrition as a result of growing wealth in Europe and America during the past 200 years is responsible in large part for this increase in physical proportions. Although birth weights have remained almost the same during the past 300 years, growth after birth has accelerated in the twentieth century in all countries of the West and in some Asiatic countries. American children, for example, are maturing physically and sexually six months to two years earlier than their parents did, and almost three years earlier than a century ago.

The effects of nutrition on physical development were dramatically illustrated in the summer of 1968 in New Delhi, when India held track and field tryouts to select a team to represent it in the Olympic Games. Not a single Indian man or woman met the minimum qualifying standards required to participate in any of the thirty-two track-and-field events in Mexico City. Lack of public support for athletics and outdated training techniques were no doubt partly responsible for this poor showing, but poor nourishment was certainly a large factor. In rural areas of India, as many as four out of five preschool children suffer from malnutritional dwarfism.

Protein is as important for mental development as it is for physical development. Protein shortages in the early years of life impair the growth of the brain and the central nervous system, thus preventing the realization of genetic potential and permanently reducing learning capacity. The relationship between nutrition and mental development was strikingly shown in a recent study conducted over several years in Mexico. An experimental group of thirty-seven children who had been hospitalized with severe protein malnutrition before the age of five was found to average thirteen points lower in intelligence quotient than a carefully selected control group who had not experienced severe malnutrition. Reports from Czechoslovakia and Japan have also supported the link between nutrition and mental development. Unfortunately, the effects of malnutrition are lasting. No amount of compensatory feeding, education, or environmental improvement in later life can repair the damage to the central nervous system. Today, protein shortages are depreciating the stock of human resources—the most vital and valuable resources on the planet—for at least a generation to come.

Malnutrition also directly and indirectly causes death, particularly among the young in poor countries of Africa, Asia, and Latin America, where 50 percent of all deaths occur among children under six' years of age. In Zambia, 260 of every 1,000 babies die before their first birthday. In India and Pakistan, the number is 140 in every 1,000; in Colombia, it is 82. Many others die before reaching school age, and more die during early school years.

Since malnutrition reduces the body's ability to resist disease, even minor ailments can be fatal to a severely malnourished child. The common infectious diseases of childhood are often catastrophic in poor areas of the world. In contrast, most children in America shrug off measles, chicken pox, whooping cough, and other childhood diseases in an almost routine way. Where death certificates are issued for preschool children in the poor countries, death is generally attributed to measles, pneumonia, dysentery, or some other disease. Basically, these children are likely to be victims of malnutrition. Thus death due to measles is 100 times greater in Bolivia and Chile than in North America. In Ecuador, it is 300 times greater.

All in all, it has been estimated that 10,000 people die each day all over the world from malnutrition, either directly or indirectly. Although this estimate cannot be confirmed, it may be reasonable. But the number could be far greater.

Stanford biologist Paul Ehrlich wants to redefine the meaning of death by malnutrition and starvation. He suggests attributing to malnutrition any death that would have been avoided if the person had been given a fully adequate diet. If this could be done with reasonable accuracy, it would make clearer the suffering and social costs of malnutrition.

Many living in perpetual malnutrition do not die in childhood. They live on and suffer from lack of vitality and from poor health. The listlessness and lack of motivation sometimes thought to be cultural may be attributed more to malnutrition than to any other single factor.

The problem of malnutrition is inseparable from the problem of poverty. Traditional food habits, lack of nutritional education, internal parasites, and ecological constraints contribute to malnutrition; but these are in many ways simply additional manifestations of poverty. Even in the United States, malnutrition is often found where there is poverty—among migrant workers and many poor inhabitants of Appalachia, parts of the rural South, and urban slums. The connection is impossible to ignore in the poor countries. The *World Food Budget* shows that the 1.1 billion people living in diet-adequate regions had an average yearly income of $1,070 per person; the 1.9 billion in diet-deficit countries had an average income of $97. Malnutrition is fundamentally an economic problem. Where income is low, cheap energy food such as cassava, potatoes, and cereals completely dominate the diet, often accounting for 60 to 80 percent of total calorie intake. The availability of protein-rich livestock products is usually quite low in these circumstances, and protein deficiencies are commonplace.

Although many promising ways of solving the huge problem of hunger have been suggested, the surest way to raise nutritional standards is to raise incomes (Figures 2 and 3). Diets improve most rapidly where per capita incomes are growing fastest, as in Europe, Japan, Mexico, and Taiwan. In the course of history, rising incomes have been associated with improvements of diet. Only during recent years has overeating or overnutrition come to be a pervasive nutritional problem for the large fraction of mankind who have not learned to adapt to abundance. Overnutrition is, in fact, the most common form of malnutrition in the prosperous Western countries. In the United States, as many as 10-15 million people may be undernourished, but it is believed that several times this number suffer from overnutrition. Overnutrition may be a major rea-

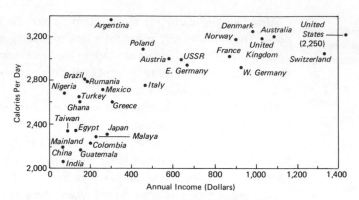

figure 2. *Income and food energy supply per person. (From U.S. Department of Agriculture.)*

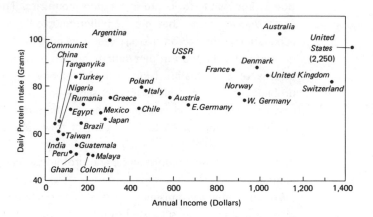

figure 3. *Income and total protein supply per person. (From U.S. Department of Agriculture.)*

son why life expectancy has not increased in the United States over the past decade. Because this modern nutritional problem is sufficiently recent, few, if any, governments have policies to deal with overnutrition while many have policies to deal with problems of undernutrition.

SUGGESTED READINGS

Berg, Alan, "Malnutrition and National Development," *Foreign Affairs*, October, 1967.

history, geography, and economics of malnutrition

Borgstrom, Georg, *The Hungry Planet*, New York: Macmillan, 1965.

Food and Agriculture Organization of the United Nations, *Protein: At the Heart of the World Food Problem*, Rome: United Nations, 1964.

Food and Agriculture Organization of the United Nations, *Third World Food Survey*, Rome, Freedom from Hunger Campaign, Basic Study, no. 11, 1963.

Freeman, Orville F., *World Without Hunger*, New York: Praeger, 1968.

Hardin, Clifford M., ed., *Overcoming World Hunger*, Englewood Cliffs, N.J.: Prentice-Hall, 1969.

Hunger USA, Report by the Citizens' Board of Inquiry into Hunger and Malnutrition in the United States, Boston: Beacon Press, 1968.

Masefield, Geoffrey Bussell, *Famine: Its Prevention and Relief*, London: Oxford University Press, 1963.

Paddock, William, and Paul Paddock, *Hungry Nations*, Boston: Little, Brown, 1967.

President's Science Advisory Committee, *The World Food Problem*, Report of the Panel on the World Food Supply, 3 vols., Washington, D.C.: U.S. Government Printing Office, 1967.

The World Food Budget of 1970, Economic Research Service, Foreign Agricultural Economic Report, no. 19, U.S. Department of Agriculture, Washington, D.C.: U.S. Government Printing Office, 1965.

2
origins
of
agriculture

Man may have first appeared in the thin film of life encircling the earth as early as 2 million years ago, which is very recent in geologic time. Throughout most of his existence, his food supply has tended to limit his numbers. For hundreds of thousands of years (more than 99 percent of his existence), he hunted and gathered wild food, living as a predator, scavenger, and primitive food collector. Because his life was largely a search for food, his campsites were impermanent, and starvation was a constant threat. Surviving on wild food necessitated, for the most part, living in small groups and wandering over considerable land areas, migrating with the prey and with the seasons. While he depended entirely on hunting and gathering, his numbers probably never exceeded 10 million, the estimated human population that the earth could support under those conditions, a population smaller than that of London or Afghanistan today.

Then somehow, perhaps as recently in man's existence as 10,000–12,000 years ago, he learned to domesticate animals and plants and began the great transition from hunter to tiller. At first only a handful of men were attracted to the new, more settled agrarian way of life; but over the millennia, it has become the preferred way of life. Today only a small fraction of 1 percent of the human race continues to live by hunting. The transition from hunter to tiller is virtually complete. Man has substituted the vagaries of weather for the uncertainty of the hunt.

Even before agriculture developed, man spread around the world to all continents except Antarctica. But predators such as lions and man the hunter remained, by force of the conditions of their existence, relatively scarce and sparse in the uncontrolled balance of nature. With the domestication of animals and plants, man began to shape the earth's ecosystem to his own ends. Man the hunter, even with the use of fire for perhaps a million years, had an exceedingly limited capacity for intervening in his environment. But man the tiller developed a seemingly endless capacity for altering his environment, multiplying his numbers in the process.

Initially quite simple and limited to a few small areas of the planet, man's interventions in nature in his quest for food became successively more complex and widespread. Eventually some of his interventions were to exceed his understanding of them, creating worrisome problems, both in the past and increasingly today. Some of these problems are largely local; but others, the more serious ones, are global in scale.

In simplest terms, agriculture is an effort by man to move beyond the limits set by nature and to shape his environment to better suit his needs. With the invention of agriculture, man set in motion a flow of events that was literally to alter the face of the earth, an alteration that continues today and at an accelerating pace. Man selected a handful of crops and a few species of animals that in nature had been useful to him as sources of food and clothing. He began to favor and protect them, discriminating against their competitors and enemies, thereby changing the relative abundance and distribution of the planet's plant and animal life. Eventually man and his domesticates were to dominate the earth.

Cows, first domesticated in the Middle East, were to spread with man to the four corners of the earth. They were eventually to populate the grassy Pampas of Argentina; displace the massive herds of bison (once numbering an estimated 30–40 million) in North America; compete with the zebra, gazelle, and other hoofed animals for the grass of the East African plateau; fill the great river valleys of Asia; replace the reindeer in Europe; and take over the kangaroo territory of Australia. Hundreds of millions of acres of forest land were to be burned and cleared and planted to crops that better met man's needs. Grassland on which wild animals grazed was to be plowed and planted to grasses that had large seeds (wheat, barley, rye, oats, rice, millets) easily consumable by man. Today, wheat alone covers 600 million acres of land that once supported wild grasses and forest, an area equivalent to the region of the United States east of the Mississippi, or nearly a million square miles.

Although the origins of agriculture are still a mystery just currently being unraveled, some of the earliest evidence of the revolutionary change in man's role from hunter and food collector to herdsman and tiller is found in western Asia, in the hills and grassy northern plains surrounding the Fertile Crescent. It is the region bordering the drainage basin of the Tigris–Euphrates, an area of hilly uplands building toward the higher mountains of Iran, Iraq, Turkey, Syria, and Palestine. Climate was hospitable there, providing generous winter and spring rainfall to revive grasses that had withered in the summer drought. Food resources were relatively abundant. Wheat, barley, peas, and lentils grew wild there; and there were sheep, goats, pigs, cattle, asses and deer, gazelles, horses, and dogs. To this day, wild barley and two kinds of wild wheat (emmer and einkorn) flourish in the region, as do wild goats, sheep, and pigs.

Sometime after 10,000 B.C., groups of hunters and food gatherers living in the hills around the Fertile Crescent began to move out of their caves to semipermanent encampments and, in some places, to more permanent sites or hunting villages. People living in most of these camps and settlements still hunted or collected most of their food. But the presence of sickles (the earliest known examples of distinctly agricultural implements) and mortars, as well as the large increase proportionally in bones of wild animal species capable of domestication (sheep, goats, cattle, horses) compared with older sites having great numbers of wild deer and gazelle bones, and caches of wild cereal grain indicate that man was intensively collecting food, that he was perhaps experimenting with domestication, and that certainly, although incidentally, he was accumulating experience and familiarity with the species he eventually did domesticate. The invention of agriculture in southwestern Asia took place in this context of the intensified or stepped-up collection of wild food by people making the transition from cave dweller to villager, hinting at a change of consciousness or a conscious effort to produce food.

Available evidence indicates that in western Asia, animals were domesticated before plants, making the earliest agrarians there herdsmen. Bones of sheep identified as domesticates dating back to around 9000 B.C. were found at an open-air encampment, Zawi Chemi, in northeastern Iraq; this makes sheep the earliest known domesticates. To most zoologists, the domesticated animal is the animal comfortable enough in association with man to be able to reproduce in captivity. In a cave near Zawi Chemi, animal bones showed that the cave's inhabitants had hunted mainly wild goats and less often wild sheep during the late Ice Age. Then, at a time coinciding with the shift from cave to open site, the composition of animal bones changed. Sheep bones began to outnumber goat bones by around sixteen to one. And the proportion of bones of young animals or yearlings increased from about 25 percent to 60 percent of the total. This high proportion indicates domestication. Presumably man was husbanding sheep and slaughtering yearlings for food.

Whether Zawi Chemi and similar encampments were occupied by man year round or only seasonally is not yet determined. They may have been merely staging posts on the route from summer to winter pastures. Early herdsmen frequently followed a rather pastoral, often nomadic way of life, similar in many ways to that characterizing significant fractions of populations in the Middle East, Afghanistan, and parts of

Africa north and south of the Sahara today, 10,000–12,000 years later.

Man's initial environmental intervention as a result of his efforts to control animals as an assured source of food was modest. Man probably herded or controlled a few animals of any one or several species still wild, protecting them from other predators for his own future use. There is some suggestion from at least one prehistoric encampment in Iraq that wild goats were being herded. But herding or even taming wild species does not constitute domestication. The principle underlying domestication, for both animals and plants, is control by man of reproduction.

No one knows just how man domesticated food animals. Perhaps tamer adult animals approached humans in search of food, remaining because they were fed and eventually reproducing. Or perhaps man brought lambs or kids, and later calves, colts, and so forth, back from the hunt as pets or future decoys to be used in hunting. These animals, raised and perhaps even nursed by humans, may have reproduced until, in time, the nucleus of a herd was formed. Through selecting the more manageable individuals, man would have gradually developed submissive herds.

Goats and pigs were domesticated next, goats definitely before 7500 B.C. Cattle were domesticated later, perhaps as early as 6000 B.C. and certainly by 5000 B.C. The date for horses is more recent than the date for cattle, but domestication was certainly accomplished long before 3500 B.C. Evidence on the dog, which was an early domesticate in southwestern Asia and elsewhere, is even less clear. Sheep, goats, and cattle were raised primarily for meat and hides. Wild sheep had hair, not wool; it took time to develop wool-bearing sheep. Wild and early domesticated cattle gave little milk. Only much later, as a result of man's selecting, favoring, and breeding efforts, did milk-producing strains emerge. Man, even thousands of years after the cow had been domesticated, had great difficulty making them lactate at times other than while nursing offspring.

A proliferation of types and varieties has followed the domestication of animals. Man has improved species through selecting animals with desired traits, breeding and cross breeding them, developing strains to serve specific food purposes. For example, today man has a variety of breeds of dairy cattle and a number of breeds of beef cattle. He has developed chickens specialized for egg production and other types specialized for broiler production.

Wheat and barley were probably the first plants domesticated in southwestern Asia, although peas and lentils may also have been cultivated as early. The oldest positive remains of wheat and barley come from full-fledged farming villages like Jarmo, in northeastern Iraq, and date from around 7000 B.C. But the standard of domestication reached and the strains of crops grown suggest a long prehistory of plant cultivation, selection, and evolution that also may have reached back into the ninth millennium B.C.

In the period of stepped-up food collection before man consciously planted seeds, he harvested wild cereal plants and stored amounts of grain, which in itself was a change from vagabond gathering tradition. Man may also have gradually learned to assist the growth of wild food plants by pulling out competing plants. Present-day experiments with wild einkorn wheat in southwestern Asia have shown that one man can gather more than 4 pounds of grain in an hour using a flint sickle. This amount threshes out, in a wooden mortar and pestle, to 2 pounds of clean grain. It is estimated that a prehistoric family working for three weeks of a normal harvest could have acquired about a ton of clean grain, perhaps enough for a year's supply.

Heads of wild cereal plants burst open upon ripening fully. Their rather fragile seed-holding spikes become brittle and drop the grains, allowing them to scatter. Among wild cereal plants, however, some which have recessive genes have tougher spikes and are, consequently, of a nonscattering variety. The grains hang on. These wild cereal plants appear to have been the ones harvested with flint sickles before domestication. Eventually their seeds were the ones planted.

It is more than likely that women were the inventors of plant cultivation. In hunting and fishing societies everywhere, women are the food gatherers, the foragers, the seekers of seeds and roots, nuts and fruits. They had, consequently, better opportunities for observing the relation between seeds accidently dropped and the subsequent germination. Planting, weeding, and harvesting are still women's jobs today in most nonliterate societies, such as those found in East Africa. It is only when agriculture becomes a major job, displacing hunting and fishing or herding as the major economic activity, that men take over farming. It is probable that men were the herders in early farming communities and women the field cultivators, perhaps until man hitched plows to draft animals and followed them into grain fields.

By at least 6000 B.C., when the greatest part of the human race was still living by hunting, fishing, and gathering, village communities, supported mainly by farming and averaging 200–500 individuals, had fully matured in southwestern Asia. The discovery in 1965 of an early farming village on the Macedonian plain in northern Greece revealed that agriculture and its more settled way of life had also reached into southeastern Europe during the seventh millennium B.C. Such agricultural villages, indicating a transition from caves to settled farming life, appear to have stretched across a 2,500-mile zone from Afghanistan in the east to Macedonia or Greece in the west. Before 5000 B.C., this agrarian way of life was moving down into the alluvial river plains of the Tigris–Euphrates valley in the south.

Early village farming communities raised wheat, barley, often lentils, sheep, goats, and perhaps pigs and cattle. It was a mixed agricultural economy of herd animals and cereal cultivation. Differences among the early farming communities were mainly a matter of emphasis, not of kind, some perhaps favoring pastoralism and others field cropping. But mixed farming, combining stock raising with crop cultivation, became the distinguishing characteristic of agriculture in western Asia and Europe.

A fully developed nomadic pastoralism eventually diverged from Neolithic mixed agriculture, spreading into the enormous grassy plains, steppes, and deserts of central Asia, stretching

from Europe to China and into northern Arabia; but that came
later.

In time, knowledge of farming spread throughout the world.
It moved eastward across Asia, southward into the Tigris–
Euphrates, then along the Nile into Africa, and northwestward
into Europe through the Danube valley and along the Mediterranean coast. By around 3000 B.C., all the plains lying south
of the Scandinavian mountains were inhabited by settlers living in more or less permanent villages. They were cultivating a
variety of crops; raising goats, sheep, cattle, and pigs; and cutting the deciduous forest with stone axes. Hunting was already
of small importance. By 1500 B.C., the last hunting stronghold
of western Eurasia was the subarctic zone of tundra and co-
niferous forest extending right across northern Eurasia from
the Norwegian coasts eastward.

Agriculture apparently had independent origins in the Americas, with cultivation centers in the Andean highlands, in the
Amazon basin, and in Middle America. This opinion is not held
universally. Some feel that the idea, at least, of agriculture
spread across land and sea, reaching America through either
migration across the Bering Strait or voyages across the Pacific.
But it is certain that beans and squash were being cultivated in
the New World 9,000 years ago. Agriculture probably originated independently in southeastern Asia as well. The diver-
gence between grain-centered field agriculture of southwestern
Asia, which depended upon planting seeds, and the root-grow-
ing style of monsoon Asia, which depended upon transplanting
offshoots from a parent plant, supports this thesis. There are
current claims that agriculture evolved earlier in the area of
Thailand than in southwestern Asia. Evidence is accumulating
which indicates that man was cultivating rice in Thailand
12,000 years ago. Whether agriculture in China began independently or by diffusion from southwestern or southeastern Asia
is still an open question. Many experts feel that the agricultural techniques and domesticated species from western and
monsoon Asia met and mingled in northern China in the Yellow River valley sometime in the third millennium B.C.

By the time of the Industrial Revolution, agriculture had

swept the world, and hunting had long since been adandoned by almost all mankind. The few hunters who remain today— the Bushmen of South Africa; the natives of Australia, of the Andaman Islands in the Bay of Bengal, and of Tierra del Fuego at the tip of South America; and the inhabitants of the arctic regions of Siberia and America—are remote and isolated from the rest of the world. These hunters, living on what they can catch and find on deserts, barren grounds, and icy lands, have survived with remarkable ingenuity and adaptibility because they had what no one else wanted.

The food plants (such as wheat, barley, rice, corn, and potatoes) domesticated earliest by man in Old and New World centers of origin fill contemporary farm fields and remain man's staple crops. More than 3,000 years ago, by 1500 B.C., man was cultivating all the major food staples grown today. With the exception of tomatoes and coffee, man has domesticated no important new food plants in the last 2,000 years. Man lives on relatively few of the 500,000–1,000,000 plant species extant on the planet.

Similarly, the first animals to be domesticated for the purposes of food (sheep, goats, cattle, pigs) remain man's major food animals. In ancient Egypt, attempts to domesticate deer and gazelles were unsuccessful, as were nineteenth-century attempts to domesticate zebras.

Today the composition of the global farmyard consists of about as many animals as people: around 3.5 billion, almost two-thirds of which are cattle and sheep, forming populations of just over 1 billion each. Fewer than half a billion goats and just over half a billion pigs are found in the global farmyard. Camels (12 million), asses (42 million), and mules (15 million) are the least-numerous farmyard animals. There are roughly twice as many water buffaloes (121 million) as horses (62 million). The horse is the only species declining in numbers. All other species are increasing, pigs most rapidly. The pig population has doubled since 1950. Asia, with almost a third of the farmyard population, has more livestock than any other continent.

For hunting groups, almost the whole of life was spent fol-

origins of
agriculture

lowing animals preyed upon, moving from one berry patch to another, living now in this cave, now in that cave, or perhaps in a few half-buried shelters such as those in prehistoric eastern Europe. There were no permanent villages, no woven cloth, no pottery, no utensils, and no time for much of anything except protection and the quest for food. Very few were freed from hunting.

The great Neolithic achievements of cultivation and husbandry gave man a more abundant and secure food supply, allowing him to break out of the limits on number and density (and life-style) set by unmanaged nature, making possible an immediate and continuing increase in his numbers. The number and size of agricultural villages attest to the remarkable growth in population attending the initial enlargement of the food supply. Agriculture established the basis for permanent settlement and civilization. Certainly the whole history of civilized man would have been impossible without the enlargement of the human food supply through man's conscious control of plants and animals. Agriculture eventually made possible the formation of cities and the concentration of large numbers of people, removing older limits to social change. Grain fields and herds fed the growing urban populations of man's earliest civilizations—those of the Tigris–Euphrates valley and of the Nile valley—sometime after 4000 B.C. Later they supported early cities on Crete, in the Indus valley of western India, and in the Yellow River valley.

Even if achievement of agriculture did not predetermine them, subsequent developments followed quickly. Although man had existed for at least 2 million years, the invention of agriculture and the rise of early civilizations occurred within a few thousand years of one another, which is very rapid in geologic time. This is no coincidence. In a hunting society very few people were freed from the quest for food. The ability to produce food and store it in granaries and on the hoof released some men, albeit a small minority, from the incessant search for sustenance. Although the surplus was never large, agricultural workers were able to produce more food than they alone required. This surplus was used to support specialists in other occupations—traders, artisans, priests, soldiers, toolmakers, officials—and, to a limited degree, for trade. Organized projects such as the building of roads, temples, irrigation canals, and harbors were carried out. As agriculture advanced over the centuries, more and more men were freed from the land. Newer centers of commerce and learning sprang up. Eventually came the Industrial Revolution and modern society. Man in today's advanced nations is able to feed a whole population with as little as 5 percent of his numbers tilling the land.

Even as a hunter, man had become the most inventive and adaptive of animals. But social and cultural evolution and economic development had occurred incredibly slowly. The invention of agriculture wrought a radical shift in man's relation to his environment. He was no longer a mere predator. He began to shape his world, to recreate it, and at an accelerating pace. After 2 million or more years of wandering and preying upon his environment, man took a step with the domestication and control of his food sources that was to enable him to go from the cave to the moon within 12,000 years.

Nevertheless, the problem of obtaining enough food remained. A succession of technological advances such as the discovery of irrigation and the harnessing of draft animals for food production has expanded the earth's food-producing capacity. Spurts in food production have permitted man's numbers to increase, and these increases have in turn exerted pressure on the food supply, forcing man to innovate and devise still more effective means of producing food. These two mutually reinforcing factors have brought man to the point where he must attempt to arrest the vicious cycle before, as will be discussed in Chapters 12 and 13, the agricultural stresses on the earth's ecosystem become too great.

SUGGESTED READINGS

Braidwood, Robert J., "The Agricultural Revolution," *Scientific American*, September, 1960.

Curwen, Eliot C., and Gudmund Hatt, *Plough and Pasture, The Early History of Farming*, New York: Crowell Collier and Macmillan, 1961.

origins of
agriculture

Hawkes, Jacquetta, and Sir Leonard Woolley, *Prehistory and the Beginnings of Civilization*, History of Mankind, vol. 1, New York: Harper & Row, 1962.

McNeill, William H., *The Rise of the West: A History of the Human Community*, New York: New American Library, 1965.

Rodden, Robert J., "An Early Neolithic Village in Greece," *Scientific American*, April, 1965.

Sauer, Carl O., *Agricultural Origins and Dispersals*, Cambridge, Mass.: M.I.T. Press, 1969.

Young, T. Cuyler, Jr., and Philip E. L. Smith, "Research in the Prehistory of Central Western Iran,"*Science*, July 22, 1966.

3
what
man eats

Man has inherited the long gastrointestinal tract of the herbivore and the dentition of the carnivore, but he is everywhere an omnivore. He is capable of eating, and does eat, almost anything edible that grows on this planet, even the most poisonous plants and animals, once the poison is removed. The Australian aborigine, for example, thinks nothing of catching a poisonous snake with his foot, picking it up, biting off its head, skinning it, and then downing it. For millennia in Latin America and for centuries in Africa, man has prepared and eaten as a dietary staple the bitter manioc plant, which is toxic in the raw state. Even before man knew how to produce his own food, his omnivorous nature enabled him to inhabit all the diverse environments of the globe where plant and animal life, regardless of kind, were plentiful enough to keep him alive.

Pre-agricultural man's food habits may have resembled those of the Kalahari Desert Bushmen in South Africa, one of today's few remaining hunting groups. Bushmen think almost exclusively about food and spend their lives hunting for it, living as parasites on wild flora and fauna, and often competing with other animals, such as the cheetah, for it. Their ability to adapt to and exploit the food resources of their rather harsh environment is remarkable, but not atypical of hunters. Although they prefer wild vegetables and the flesh of certain game animals such as the antelope, they will eat anything they can digest—rats, lions, snakes, hyenas, lizards, frogs, insects, scorpions, grubs, and the available seeds, berries, wild plums, wild melons, wild veld cabbage, and many bulbs and roots. They are not particular about the state of their food and are able to eat meat that is putrid or ostrich eggs already old and smelly. They can also endure the rhythm of feast and famine, eating prodigiously whenever food is abundant, surviving on short rations when necessary, or going completely without food for considerable periods. In half a day, two Bushmen are able to consume a whole sheep or comparable amounts of wild game—intestines and all. This voracious and indiscriminate eating is typical of hunting groups.

Until 12,000 years ago, all human populations lived by hunting and often by fishing, supplementing their diets with berries, fruits, nuts, roots, and tubers. Animal ossuaries (great pits or piles of bones) left by man the hunter from France to Russia attest to the importance of meat in pre-agricultural diets. Ten thousand or more horse skeletons were found at one Paleolithic site at Solutré, France, and almost a thousand mammoth skeletons at Predmost, Czechoslovakia. Animals were often killed by stampeding them over steep river banks or cliffs. But man had also developed good hunting tools, and he used fire in the chase.

Probably the most significant change in mankind's diet since the start of agriculture is the great shift in importance from animal to vegetable food sources. Livestock products and fish now supply only 12 percent of man's current global food energy supply. In some parts of the planet, this proportion is much higher; and in other parts, it is much lower. Today only four countries, all wealthy, derive more calories from livestock than from starchy foods: Canada, the United States, Australia, and New Zealand.

Man eats various parts of plants: leaves, stems, roots, seeds, fruit, blossoms. Some plants such as beet, turnip, and taro (a potato-like vegetable that serves as a mainstay of diets in the islands of the South Pacific) are consumed almost wholly. For example, the root of the taro is either baked or boiled, eaten whole, or made into paste; and its leaves or foliage are consumed as a green vegetable. The leaves and stems of many plants are used as spices. With a vegetable such as spinach, both the leaves and stems are consumed, but the roots are not. With grape plants, the fruit and leaves are used as food, but the roots and stems are not. Blossoms of pumpkin plants are stuffed with cheese and meat fillings and consumed by man. Seeds are, however, by far the most important plant part in the global diet. Man eats the seeds of many kinds of plants: pea, bean, sesame, sunflower, pumpkin, caraway, celery, and so forth. But cereals, which are grasses with large seeds, alone provide 53 percent of man's food energy when consumed directly and a sizable part of the remainder when eaten indirectly in the form of animal products based on feed grains.

Wheat and rice, both domesticated in the Old World, are the dominant staples of mankind (Figure 4). They each contribute almost a fifth of man's calorie intake. Wheat, the most widely cultivated and heavily traded cereal, is grown and consumed in nearly every country in the world. It is the principal staple in almost all high-income countries, as well as in some poorer

figure 4. *Man's sources of food energy. (From U.S. Department of Agriculture.)*

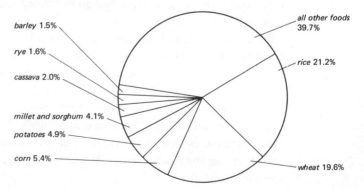

barley 1.5%

rye 1.6%

cassava 2.0%

millet and sorghum 4.1%

potatoes 4.9%

corn 5.4%

all other foods 39.7%

rice 21.2%

wheat 19.6%

countries such as Algeria, Morocco, Egypt, Tunisia, Libya, and the countries of its ancient homeland (Iran, Israel, Jordan, Lebanon, Syria, and Turkey). All in all, forty-three countries, containing about a third of the human population, depend upon wheat as their primary starchy staple.

In contrast with wheat, rice is the principal food for most of the world's poor. Although it is the major staple in only sixteen of the world's countries, these countries, mainly Asian, contain more than half the world's population. Furthermore, rice-eating areas are more heavily dependent upon rice for food energy than wheat-eating areas are on wheat. Half of mankind depends on rice alone for close to 50 percent of their daily calorie intake; whereas in wheat-eating areas, wheat alone supplies a much smaller proportion of the total food energy intake. An acre of rice yields almost twice as much food energy as an acre of wheat. It is no accident, therefore, that apart from industrial areas, the largest concentrations of human population on the planet are in rice-growing regions.

Corn, man's third-ranking staple food, supplies more than 5 percent of man's food energy and is the leading food staple of fourteen countries, including most of the Central American nations, as well as Bolivia, Venezuela, and Colombia in South America and Kenya, South Africa, Angola, and Rhodesia in Africa. Other cereals such as millet, sorghum, and rye together contribute around 7 percent of man's food-energy intake. Oats are fed mainly to horses. Teff, a grass producing very small, edible seeds, is the staple food of Ethiopia, where it provides more than 50 percent of the total calorie intake. It is not widely cultivated elsewhere.

Starchy roots or short, fleshy underground stems are next in importance to seeds among man's dominant plant foods. Potatoes, including white potatoes, sweet potatoes, yams, and cocoa yams, give man around 5 percent of his food energy. Only in Africa (in Ghana and Nigeria), are populations dependent upon potatoes as their major food support. Another root, cassava, supplying around 2 percent of man's calorie consumption, is the dominant staple in three Latin American countries (Brazil, Haiti, and Paraguay) and in four African nations (Belgian Congo, Ruanda-Urundi, Togoland, and Cameroon).

Sugar, obtained from the stalks of the sugarcane plant in tropical and semitropical countries and from the roots of the sugar beet in temperate countries, supplies more calories than any other food in Costa Rican and Dominican Republic diets. Fruits, namely bananas and plantains, are also exceptionally important in the Dominican Republic. Uganda also relies largely on bananas as a staple. All in all, cereals, potatoes, cassava, and sugar account for more than 70 percent of man's food-energy intake. Nuts, fruits, and vegetables provide more than 9 percent of man's total calorie supply; and fats and oils, just under 9 percent. As mentioned earlier, livestock products and fish furnish the remaining 12 percent.

Historically, most of the world's cereal crop has been consumed directly. Eating cereals in the forms of bread, pudding, and porridge (if not of Marie Antoinette's cake) was the earliest and least costly way to sustain the earth's poor and multiplying peasants. Since the Industrial Revolution, and particularly in recent decades, more and more of the global cereal crop has been fed to animals. Many speculate that whereas now most cereal is eaten directly by man, within a few decades a major share of the crop could be consumed by livestock, provided that human fertility is brought under control and that the earth's ecosystem is preserved.

Some cereals are used predominantly as food grains in certain areas of the world and as feed grains in others. Corn is used largely for livestock feed in North America, where just over half the world's supply is grown. In Africa and Latin America, it is used principally as human food. Sorghum is a food grain in Africa and a feed grain in the United States and Europe. In low-income India, even with a very diversified grain economy producing millet, rice, wheat, sorghum, and corn, almost all the grain is eaten by humans. This was true in Mexico, another diversified grain producer, until recent years; but now a growing proportion of the cereal crop is being fed to animals.

Since the beginning of domestication, man has intervened more and more in the natural cycles of animals, developing livestock to suit his specific food wants. Originally man took eggs laid by hens for reproductive purposes and used them for food. Then, over time, he worked to increase the egg-laying capacity of poultry. He planted decoys in chicken's nests, for example, to foster the nesting instinct and coax the hen to produce more than the normal clutch, 15 eggs per year. He began to select and breed good producers, eventually developing chickens that yielded more eggs than were necessary to preserve the species. Today the nesting instinct has been bred out of chickens in many parts of the world. The early ancestors of our current hen probably did not lay more than 15 eggs per year. Last year the average American hen laid 220 eggs. The world record is held by an industrious Japanese hen that laid 365 eggs in one year. Agricultural scientists at Beltsville, Maryland, are now trying to outfox the hens by reducing the length of the day through controlled lighting.

Man has also intervened in the natural cycles of cows and other animals in order to acquire more milk, using methods both ingenious and deceitfully cunning. The first cattle domesticated probably did not produce more than 600 pounds of milk per year, the average produced by cows in India today and barely enough to support a calf to the point where it could forage for itself. In antiquity, man often used a decoy calf to encourage a cow to lactate when it was not nursing a calf. Sometimes he dressed himself in hides and pretended to be a calf. He often stroked the cow's genitals or blew in its vagina to stimulate lactation. Through centuries of selecting and breeding, man gradually developed dairy cows able to produce much more milk than necessary to sustain a calf for the year intended by nature. Modern dairy cows in the United States produce 8,000 pounds of milk per year, or ten to twenty times the amount produced by the ancient ancestors. A recent article on the society pages of the Washington *Evening Star*, entitled "She's Contented and Liberated," reported that a Maryland cow, Rheinharts Ballad, had produced a new world record of 42,000 pounds of milk in the 365-day period. This amounts to 49 quarts a morning on the doorstep, or seventy times more than her early ancestors.

These advances in animal breeding have environmental consequences, since the new genetic potentials can be realized only through altering livestock diets. Efficient, high-powered producers make possible much higher levels of protein intake in man's diet, but they require large amounts of concentrated nutrients in the form of cereals and protein-rich feedstuffs such as soybeans and fish meal along with their traditional intake of roughage. Consequently, a large proportion of the earth's agricultural land is put under the plow and converted from grassland to cropland in order to produce the necessary feed. And perhaps one-half of the oceanic fish catch is converted into fish meal for animals. Much of the Peruvian fish catch is sent to the United States and Western Europe, where it is consumed indirectly in the form of poultry, meat, and eggs.

What man eats is influenced by where he lives, what he earns, and what his customs and religious beliefs are. Which principal staples he consumes are determined more by geography than by income or custom. If he lives in monsoon Asia, his staple food will most likely be rice. If he lives in Latin America or East Africa, the chances are that it will be corn. And if he resides in Europe or North America, it will be wheat.

But if he lived in North America or Europe two or more centuries ago, his dominant food would more than likely have been rye or barley or oats, which are higher-yielding and, therefore, cheaper to produce than wheat. As incomes began to rise over the past 200 years in the northern countries of Europe and in North America, wheat became the dominant staple there: Wheat is the staple cereal of the rich.

Diets of the poor tend to be limited and monotonous, consisting of a high proportion of starchy foods and a low proportion of animal products. Where incomes are low—as in Asia, Africa, and Latin America—cheap energy foods such as grains completely dominate man's consumption pattern. And the lower the income, the cheaper and starchier the staple. In Japan, for example, rice is the dominant staple, but the more inexpensive and starchier yam or sweet potato has in the past been the food of poorer groups. Only Israel and Singapore are exceptions to extreme dependence throughout Asia on starchy staples. Even Japan, with a relatively high standard of living otherwise, still depends upon starches for close to two-thirds of its energy supply.

Man has always associated wealth and the good life with an increase in the variety and quality of his diet. Until approximately two centuries ago, the majority of agricultural mankind ate mainly bread or its equivalent most of the time. With the increase in wealth in industrial countries has come improvement in diet for larger and larger shares of mankind.

As man's wealth increases, animal products play a larger role in his diet. Whereas on a global scale approximately 12 percent of man's food energy consists of livestock products and fish, in North America, man consumes around 31 percent of his daily food energy in the form of meat, milk, eggs, and fish. The proportion in Western Europe is nearly 22 percent, whereas in Oceania it reaches to 36 percent. These high ratios contrast with those in Asia, where less than 5 percent of what man eats comes from livestock or fish. The rich countries of Eastern Europe and the Soviet Union have an abnormally high dependence upon starchy foods, 65 percent of the food-energy supply, while animal products contribute less than 15 percent.

In general, as incomes rise, diets become more diversified. There are five major food groups upon which man depends: starchy staples, fruits and vegetables, sugar, fats and oils, and animal products (See Table 2 and Figure 5). In North America, each of these groups supplies 16–31 percent of man's daily food energy, with the exception of fruits and vegetables, which contribute around 10 percent. A similar diversity is found in Western Europe and Oceania, while low-income regions are skewed in the direction of starchy staples. Historically, Japan held to its typical fish and rice diet, with no room in its economy for livestock development until recently. As Japanese incomes have risen since World War II, there has been a move away from the strict fish and rice pattern to a broader Western European or North American pattern. This trend to-

man and his environment: food

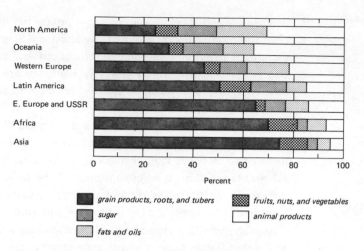

North America
Oceania
Western Europe
Latin America
E. Europe and USSR
Africa
Asia

0   20   40   60   80   100

Percent

▓ grain products, roots, and tubers   ▓ fruits, nuts, and vegetables
▓ sugar   □ animal products
▓ fats and oils

figure 5. *Distribution of major food groups by calories. (From U.S. Department of Agriculture.)*

ward diversity includes eating more wheat products as well as more livestock products, fruits, and vegetables.

Even though the United States has a very advanced and diversified agriculture, Americans still import agricultural products worth $5 billion from around the world in order to satisfy diverse tastes. The average supermarket in the United States stocks 4,000 food products.

Without advanced food-preserving techniques to slow the decaying action of enzymes and microorganisms, this desire for diversity could not be as fully satisfied. Spicing, cooking, drying, and chilling or freezing are all ancient methods of processing and preserving foods, developed and refined over time. Cooking, which allowed man the hunter to keep his meat for a week or more, has been used for perhaps 500,000 years. Drying food in the sun is at least as old as agriculture. Snow and ice were brought by the Romans from the mountains to preserve food. Steaks, 50,000 years old, cut from mammoths found frozen in Siberia and eaten by dogs and men in the twentieth century illustrate the marvelous power of cold to preserve food. In more recent times, man has added canning and chemical additives (such as sodium propionate, which is used in bread) to his arsenal of food-preserving techniques.

table 2

percentage distribution of total calorie supply by major food groups, by regions

region	grain products, roots, and tubers	fruits, nuts, and vegetables	sugar	fats and oils	livestock products	fish	total
			Percent				
Geographic regions							
North America	24.4	9.1	15.8	19.9	30.6	.2	100.0
Oceania	30.0	5.6	16.3	12.3	35.2	.6	100.0
Western Europe	43.9	6.4	11.2	16.8	20.8	.9	100.0
Latin America	50.7	12.3	14.0	8.0	14.7	.3	100.0
E. Europe & USSR	64.9	3.5	8.6	9.2	14.0	.4	100.0
Africa	70.1	11.5	4.1	7.5	6.3	.5	100.0
Asia	74.5	11.4	4.1	5.3	3.8	.9	100.0
World	62.7	9.6	7.3	8.9	10.8	.7	100.0
Economic regions							
Developed regions	47.3	5.9	11.1	14.5	20.7	.5	100.0
Less developed regions	71.7	11.5	5.1	5.8	5.1	.8	100.0

Source: U.S. Department of Agriculture.

Canning was developed by a French inventor, Nicolas Appert, around 150 years ago, after the French government offered a reward (which would be worth nearly a quarter of a million dollars today) for a practical method of preserving food in order to supply armies on the move. Today 26 billion cans and jars of food are used each year in the United States alone.

food customs and taboos

Customs and religious beliefs also influence eating patterns. Hindus, Moslems, and Jews are forbidden by religious restrictions to eat pork. In India and China, beef is eaten principally by Moslems. To the Hindus, the cow is sacred; and its slaughter is forbidden by law, although consumption of its milk is permitted. The Chinese do not drink milk, despite the presence of goats and cattle in China since ancient times. Milking was practiced all across Europe and Asia, but stopped short of the Far East and the Pacific Islands. Instead, China has developed milklike soybean products that are used extensively. The Chinese are also adept at preparing delicacies such as bird's nests and fish lips, both of which are rarely tasted by occidental man.

As in China, milking was not practiced in the tropical forests of Africa, despite the presence of animals that were milked in other parts of the world. Yet a huge sweep of cattle farmers occupy East Africa from the Nile to the southern continental tip, farmers who both milk and eat the meat of their cattle. One tribe, the Masai, are tall and lean, renowned for their physiques. They live largely on milk, as much as 4½ quarts a day, and on blood from living cattle, which is taken by shooting an arrow into the animal's jugular vein and draining it into a gourd. The fact that the diet of the Kikuyu tribe, which lives near the Masai in Tanzania, is made up almost entirely of cereals, roots, and fruits attests to the importance of custom.

Custom and taboo are also evident in the carnivorous bias of Eskimos. They have a strong distaste for eating berries and vegetables and will consume them only when in dire need. An aversion to eating dog or horse meat is identified with English-speaking people. Some nomadic peoples of Asia—the Mongols, the Kirghis, and the Kazaks—both milk and eat horses and sheep, their major food sources. Horse meat is the delicacy; sheep meat, the everyday fare. Snails, which were an important dietary item for pre-agricultural man, are today a delicacy eaten mainly by the rich, especially in France, where they are grown like livestock and consumed at the rate of 600 million a year.

Perhaps a greater conservatism and inflexibility attaches to man's food habits than to other aspects of his life. For years, Benjamin Franklin tried in vain to persuade the French to adopt the potato as a staple food. In an attempt to encourage the use of the potato in Bavaria in the late eighteenth century, soldiers were forced to cultivate and consume potatoes until they had acquired the habit and could carry it back with them to their homes. Food habits of Tunisian immigrants living in France reportedly changed long after they had adopted the French language and newspapers.

The irrational grip of habit with respect to eating patterns applies to rich and poor. Affluent Americans or Europeans, increasingly plagued by problems of obesity and overconsumption of foods potentially harmful to health, find it very difficult to alter their habits even with a full awareness of the probable consequences. In today's poorer and more traditional societies, however, the resistance to change may be even stronger, and the consequences, where malnutrition is prevalent, greater.

summary

Man's food supply comes from both land and ocean. Whether from land or sea and whether plant, animal, or plant–animal product (such as honey, wine, or cheese), it is all ultimately the product of photosynthesis. A small portion of the solar energy streaming into the earth's ecosystem is captured by green plants and stored as chemical energy. It is this chemically stored solar energy that fuels the entire animal kingdom. The microscopic plants of the sea, phytoplankton, account for almost 70 percent of the planet's photosynthetic production;

and the vegetation of the land, for around 30 percent. However, 99 percent of man's food energy comes from the land, and only 1 percent comes from the sea, although the sea supplies a much greater proportion of man's protein supply.

SUGGESTED READINGS

Brown, Lester R., *Man, Land and Food*, Washington, D.C.: U.S. Government Printing Office, 1965.

Howells, William, *Back of History*, Garden City, N.Y.: Natural History, 1963.

Sebrell, William H., Jr., and James J. Haggerty, *Food and Nutrition*, New York: Time Incorporated, 1967.

4
water
and bread

After the invention of agriculture itself, irrigation was man's next major effort to intervene in the natural functioning of the earth's ecosystem, altering it to greatly expand the earth's capacity to produce. Agricultural man discovered early, even earlier than he learned to harness animals for draft power, that he could augment limited rainfall by diverting water onto the land from rivers and streams. Man was practicing a distinctly irrigated agriculture at least as early as 6,000 years ago in the Tigris–Euphrates valley and perhaps as early as that along the Nile as well, in contrast with the predominantly rain-fed agriculture of the wooded uplands.

Irrigation is simply an intervention by man in the sun-powered natural cycling of water. In the earth's hydrologic cycle, water evaporates mainly from the oceans and other bodies of water but also from land surfaces and terrestrial plants and animals. This moisture enters and moves through the atmosphere, where it accumulates and forms clouds. Even during the driest period in any part of the earth, large masses of moisture are present in the atmosphere, drifting overhead, however invisible they may be to the naked eye. Eventually, condensation, in the forms of dew and fog, and precipitation, primarily in the form of rain but also as snow, sleet, and hail, occur. Water that falls on land and is not returned to the atmosphere through evaporation and transpiration or absorbed by plant buildup moves on to the ocean via rivers, streams, and underground pathways. To irrigate his crops, early agricultural man obstructed the flow of water that was returning to the ocean in streams and rivers, diverting the water into his fields instead. In time, he learned to pull water up from wells using water-lifting devices powered by men, animals, and wind. But in total, groundwater has been scarcely touched by man.

early uses of irrigation

Irrigation has played a great role in expanding the capacity of the earth to yield food and support growing populations. Nature distributes rainfall very unevenly over the earth, but man's modification of the hydrologic cycle has enabled him to bring into profitable cultivation vast areas of the world that would otherwise be unusable or only marginally productive, areas where the availability of water rather than the quality of land is the limiting constraint on food production. It was irrigated, not rain-fed, agriculture that provided the surplus food and spurred the social organization necessary for man's earliest civilizations in Mesopotamia and Egypt.

Mesopotamia and Egypt are lands with little or no rainfall. But in both lands, great rivers flowed, carrying rich silt from mountain sources and, over millennia, laying down a very fertile alluvium, a light, friable soil that can be worked easily with light implements. In these valleys, man did not have to shift cultivation every few years to renew depleted soil, as was the practice in the uplands. Silt depositions during periodic floods renewed the soil naturally. Man's problem was to make the rivers work for him.

Controlling the Tigris and Euphrates rivers was no easy task, since they are turbulent, often dangerous, and their floods are irregular, not predictable, and can be violent. In Mesopotamia,

water and bread

man developed a system of canals and ditches, at first simple but eventually elaborate, to control and deliver irrigation water to the fields.

Herodotus called Egypt the gift of the Nile. The Nile is a thoroughly unique river. Its flood is gentle, regular, punctual, and synchronized ideally with the natural growing season. The annual rise occurs between July and September, preparing the ground for the autumn-winter growing season. Rich, relatively salt-free silt was deposited each year by flood waters, renewing the land. And there was comparatively little silting of irrigation canals, a problem that plagued Mesopotamian irrigation. The ancient Egyptians developed a system of basins, dikes, and eventually canals to catch and regulate the flow of floodwater.

At first the earth's irrigated acreage was concentrated in the Middle East and North Africa, in the area James Breasted called the Fertile Crescent, which extends in an arc from the Persian Gulf northwestward along the Tigris and Euphrates rivers, curves southward along the eastern Mediterranean coast, and reaches into North Africa along the Nile. Irrigation expanded there, developing into complex systems capable of supporting growing populations and successive civilizations in Mesopotamia and Egypt. In the past, many areas of the Middle East, such as the Tigris-Euphrates valley, contained populations substantially larger than those that inhabit them today. Ironically, because of man's neglect and ignorance, desert sands and extremely arid conditions now prevail in much of the region.

Irrigation developed along rivers in southern Asia, particularly in the Indus system, perhaps a millennium or more later than in western Asia, and still later in eastern Asia along the Hwang Ho, or Yellow River, in China—both regions giving rise to additional ancient Oriental civilizations. Irrigation also played a significant role in supporting populations in the New World before the arrival of Europeans: in the coastal valleys of Peru, in the Incan Andes, in central Mexico, and in the North American Southwest.

Some areas of the world, notably Egypt, Mesopotamia, India, and China, have been under continuous irrigation since ancient times. Today the great bulk of the irrigated land is to be found in Asia and is devoted mainly to growing rice. China has more irrigated land than any country on earth, more than 40 percent of the world's total. China and India, the world's two most populous nations, together contain more than half the global irrigated acreage. Egypt, which, with the Sudan, has most of the irrigated land in Africa, is the only country with virtually all farmland under irrigation. Because of this, yields of Egypt's major crops have been far above those in most developing countries. The Soviet Union has the major portion of irrigated acreage in Eastern Europe. Western Europe has an abundance of rainfall, well distributed throughout the year, and therefore very little irrigated land. Spain, with its semi-arid Mediterranean climate, is an exception and has more irrigated land than all other West European countries combined.

Irrigation has played an enormous role in opening up fertile, productive regions in the Southwest of the United States to agriculture and settlement. Large areas are almost entirely dependent on irrigation. Among Western Hemisphere countries, the United States has by far the largest irrigated area. But Mexico, Argentina, Peru, and Chile also have extensive irrigated areas. Australia is unique among the continents, for unlike most great land bodies, it has no large rivers. Its potential for irrigation in the future lies in tapping underground water sources that may eventually bring into production areas of its great central desert.

In areas of little or negligible rainfall, irrigation is used to extend cultivation to land that would otherwise be uncultivable. Traditional irrigation systems were built mainly for this purpose. But irrigation is also used to intensify agriculture on already cultivated land. Most modern irrigation systems, like those in Japan or the United States, are designed to increase yield in this way.

By 1800, an estimated 20 million acres of the world's croplands were irrigated. By 1900, the total was 100 million acres. But in the twentieth century, a virtual explosion in irrigation expansion has occurred. The area irrigated has multiplied at least fourfold thus far, moving from 100 to 400 million acres between 1900 and 1965, during which period the human population jumped from 1.4 to 3.5 billion. By the year 2000, an anticipated 600–700 million acres are expected to be under irrigation. China, long the world's most populous country, increased irrigated acreage by 100 million acres in the decade of the 1950s—a phenomenal feat.

The tremendous demand for food in this century has been the major impetus for the growth in irrigated acreage. But other factors have also spurred this expansion. For one thing, the increasing availability of chemical fertilizers during the current century has raised the return on investment in the development of water resources. Also, irrigation has been an important target for investment by the World Bank and bilateral aid programs such as American assistance in irrigation development in India, Pakistan, and elsewhere and Soviet aid in the Egyptian Aswan project as well as the planned Syrian Euphrates River project. Furthermore, large-scale irrigation structures became dual-purposed or multipurposed early in the twentieth century, geared to provide hydroelectric power as well as water for crops. This development of power in conjunction with irrigation and reservoir facilities created an additional incentive to invest in irrigation works.

Rivers have always been the dominant source of water for irrigation. But man has also intervened in the hydrologic cycle by tapping surface water from ponds and groundwater from wells. In the United States, ponds located on farms have been an important source of water for small-scale irrigation systems. In Asia, bullock-driven or human-powered waterwheels have drawn water from open wells on individual farms for centuries. Withdrawing water from subterranean aquifers for irrigation has depleted those supplies in some desert areas of the world. Texas is today facing a water crisis in the High Plains, with the prospect of abandoning farmland in areas where fossil groundwater reserves are being depleted.

During recent years, there has been a significant new irrigation development in the poor countries, particularly in Asia: the widespread installation of small-scale irrigation systems on individual farms. Emphasis has shifted away from the large-scale systems that commonly form part of multipurpose TVA-like river projects. The use of tubewells (closed cylindrical shafts driven into the ground) and portable electric or diesel pumps to tap water from underground sources and low-flowing rivers has suddenly become popular with farmers. In the Indus and Gangetic plain regions of Pakistan and India, where groundwater is plentiful, where it is recharged each monsoon season, and where, in many places, it is close to the surface, hundreds of thousands of tubewells with pumps have been installed in recent years. Tubewells and pumps were introduced in the Indo-Pakistan subcontinent in the 1950s by the Agency for International Development (AID). For years, this technology was used mainly to draw groundwater for drinking, not for irrigation. But several factors, including the availability of the technology, converged in the sixties to cause the dramatic spread in the use of tubewells and pumps for small-scale irrigation.

Two drought years in South Asia in the mid-1960s, coming as they did in the context of mounting food demands and increasing dependence on external sources of food, underlined for both farmers and governments the risks of overdependence on monsoons and surface waters. Tapping groundwater resources that are independent of seasonal monsoon variations not only augments the water supply but also minimizes the risks of monsoon failure.

Farmers in countries like India and Pakistan have also turned to tubewells because huge irrigation systems, commonly forming part of multipurpose (power–irrigation–flood control) projects, have often proved inefficient. They take many years and millions of dollars to construct, tying up capital for long periods of time. Many of those begun in the fifties and early sixties have yet to come close to realizing their full irrigation potential. Seventy-two irrigation projects undertaken in India between 1951 and 1965 promised to irrigate 13.4 million hectares, but were irrigating only one-fourth of that area by 1966. And the story is similar in other countries.

Investment in multipurpose dams is usually justified in terms of power benefits rather than water. Delivering water to farmers at the right time in the right amount is a task far more complex than delivering power to a factory or community facility. After the dam is completed, canals must be built. And then effective management of the water system must evolve. But the effective delivery of irrigation waters from a large centralized system to masses of individual peasant farmers with differing water needs requires a degree of communication and orchestration not yet attainable in most poor countries.

On the more positive side, the availability of electric power in rural communities has facilitated the spread of small-scale irrigation. The cost of using electric pumps is about a third less than using diesel engines. But once farmers in electrified areas invest in pumps and engines, farmers in neighboring areas that do not have electricity tend to invest in tubewells and diesel pumps.

Although in Pakistan the use of tubewells and portable pumps in irrigation had begun during the early 1960s, particularly as part of land-reclamation efforts, the major push toward small-scale irrigation in India, Pakistan, and elsewhere came in the later 1960s with the availability of high-yielding, fertilizer-responsive, and aseasonal varieties of wheat and rice. High yields from these new plants are dependent upon generous and, in the case of rice, well-controlled water supplies, for using large quantities of fertilizer is possible only with more intensive application of water.

Traditional irrigation systems in many of the poor countries, planned and built during the nineteenth century with the help of British engineers, were essentially defensive, designed to protect crops from drought. Small amounts of water were spread thinly over large areas of land. In contrast, all modern irrigation systems, such as those in Japan or California, are intended to intensify agriculture, maximizing returns on investment. These systems will deliver five times as much water to a given land area as traditional systems.

Use of new cereal varieties combined with extremely favorable food prices in the 1960s made investment in small-scale irrigation exceedingly profitable. A farmer was able to recover his investment in a tubewell, which costs $1,000–$2,500, in as little as two years. Pakistani farmers installed 32,000 private tubewells over a five-year span in the mid-1960s. Indian farmers, during the 1968 crop year alone, installed 42,000 tubewells. Each 5,000 tubewells adds an estimated 1 million acrefeet to the yearly supply of irrigation water. The new small-scale localized irrigation projects not only bring the farmer more water but also place the water under his personal management, enabling him to control very precisely the amount and timing of the water delivered to his crops.

Governments throughout Asia are beginning to encourage small-scale irrigation financed largely by individual farmers just to reduce pressures on the national budget. All import restrictions have been removed on low-lift pumps for East Pakistan. Rural areas with underground water reserves are being given priority in electrification in India.

The use of small-scale irrigation methods that draw upon groundwater and low-flowing rivers is especially propitious because of the growing need in densely populated areas to begin farming in the dry season. Solar energy in monsoon climates is greater during the six months of the year that are very dry, with little or no rainfall. The new rice varieties, in particular, are more productive in the dry season, when there is more sunlight, assuming of course that an adequate supply of water is available. In delta areas of Thailand, South Vietnam, and East Pakistan, farmers are investing heavily in pumps to lift water from low-flowing streams and canals to field levels during the dry season. Fields once idle during that period are now green with a second crop of rice.

Although Asia has most of the planet's irrigated land, the total acreage is inadequate and the distribution is uneven. Only one-third of the region's rice land is irrigated. Most of the remaining paddy land is rain fed either by trapping monsoon rainfall in fields surrounded by low earthen dikes called *bunds* or by the annual flooding of the river floodplain from rain-swollen rivers. The water is just caught, not regulated; it cannot be moved from one field to another, and its depth cannot be raised or lowered. As agriculture is modernized and intensified, farmers keep working to achieve greater control of water. In Japan, for example, almost all water is tightly controlled.

water and bread   Man's intervention in the hydrologic cycle has extended to more and more rivers in the twentieth century and has entailed tightening control over the earth's rivers. Some river systems, such as the Colorado system in the United States, are so completely and extensively controlled for agricultural as well as for municipal and industrial purposes that little of their water ever reaches the ocean. Only a few large river systems remain relatively undisturbed: Among these are the Mekong, the Amazon, and the Congo. And substantial plans already exist for development of the Mekong.

consequences of intervention

Man has not always thoroughly understood the consequences of intervening in the hydrologic cycle. Reshaping the natural flow of water has often resulted in unwanted secondary effects or undesirable repercussions. One of these is the raising of the water table. When water, particularly from rivers, is diverted onto the land to irrigate crops, part of it is used by the plant, part evaporates into the atmosphere from the soil or from plants as they transpire, and part percolates downward. Throughout most of history, the downward percolation of water has not been taken into account in the designing of irrigation systems. Drainage has been ignored. Over time, irrigation water percolating downward and accumulating underground may gradually raise the water table until it is within a few feet or inches of the soil's surface. The rising water table brings up with it salts from ancient subterranean deposits. Once the water table rises close to the surface of the soil, two things happen: (1) Plant root systems either fail to develop or die from lack of oxygen—a problem known as *waterlogging*. (2) In addition, evaporation of water through the remaining soil leaves a deposit of salts (such as magnesium, carbonates, sulfates, and the common table salt, sodium chloride) in the topsoil that in sufficient concentrations is toxic to plants. Eventually soil may become so salty that no crops will grow and the land will have to be abandoned.

Such a situation developed in West Pakistan. Pakistan is

highly dependent upon waters of the Indus flowing from the snow-fed Himalaya Mountains across dry land to the ocean. When British engineers decided about a century ago to irrigate the arid but fertile plain by constructing barrages along the Indus River system and diverting the water onto the land, the water table was far below the soil's surface, perhaps 100 feet or more. Over decades, irrigation water percolating downward eventually brought the water table close to the surface. During President Ayub's visit to Washington in 1961, he appealed to President Kennedy for help. West Pakistan was losing 60,000 acres of fertile cropland per year because of waterlogging and salinity, while its population was expanding 2.5 percent yearly. Clearly these trends could not continue indefinitely.

An interdisciplinary team of technologists headed by Roger Revelle, then science advisor to the secretary of the interior, studied the problem in the early 1960s, using a systems approach and Harvard computers. They proposed using tubewells that would lower the water table by drawing upon groundwater to supplement river water. The additional water would allow farmers to change from traditional extensive irrigation, which spread water thinly over large land areas, to intensive irrigation. The intensive application of water, they further reasoned, would wash the soil's toxic salts downward. The plan worked, and the salty, waterlogged land is steadily being reclaimed. (The amount of land reclaimed each year now far exceeds that being lost to production.)

A look at ancient history could have provided a warning to engineers. The sequence of the diversion of river water onto land for irrigation, followed eventually by waterlogging and salinity and the abandonment of land, has been repeated many times, particularly in Mesopotamia along the Tigris and Euphrates rivers (the home of present-day Iraq). The result was invariably the decline and sometimes the disappearance of the civilizations undertaking these interventions in the hydrological system. Remains of civilizations buried beneath the desert in Mesopotamia and other parts of the Middle East attest to early experiences similar to those of contemporary Pakistan. In the New World, Incan irrigation systems were also

53

water and
bread

impaired by salinity. Archaeologists have uncovered evidence that the salting of the soil and the consequent undermining of irrigation systems or of irrigated agriculture preceded by as much as 100 years the decline of some civilizations in Mesopotamia, which was long thought by historians to have been caused primarily by the invasion of nomadic hordes or intercity warfare. They have also discovered that the progress of salinization and the northward movement of civilizations in the Tigris–Euphrates valley are highly correlated. The ancients were aware of the salinity problem. Their records show that they fallowed land as an antidote. The growth of population eventually precluded long periods of fallow, and the salt built up. Records also show that the more salt-tolerant crops like barley and dates gradually took over the cropland in the southern, saltier part of Mesopotamia, whereas the less salt-tolerant crops like wheat moved northward. American conservationist Walter Lowdermilk estimates that at its zenith, the valley supported between 17 and 25 million inhabitants. The total population of Iraq today is 8.9 million. Flying over Iraq, as well as over West Pakistan, it is possible to see miles and miles of salt-whitened land beneath, land on which crops once grew.

Waterlogging and salinity continue to plague irrigation systems along the Tigris–Euphrates and the Ganges, as well as the Indus. Egypt also has had problems of salting and rising water tables, especially in the last few years, since the Aswan has made yearlong or perennial irrigation possible. For thousands of years, the Nile valley remained remarkably free of serious salinization problems. The complex of interrelated problems in modern Egypt that have resulted from the construction of the new high dam at Aswan are all the more striking when viewed against this background.

For thousands of years, the basin system of irrigated agriculture supported civilizations and growing populations in Egypt. Then during the nineteenth century, Egyptian and European engineers began to tighten control of the Nile waters in an effort to increase agricultural production. The press of an expanding population—from 2.5 million in 1800 to 7 million in the 1880s, when plans for the first Aswan dam were conceived—as well as desire for foreign exchange from cotton increased the demand for water during spring and summer months, when cotton and second, or even third, food crops could be raised.

When the first Aswan dam was completed in 1902, there was no comparable structure anywhere in the world. The dam, together with barrages and canals located downstream, made year-round irrigation possible on large acreages. Agriculture prospered, and farmers became thirsty for yet more water. During the twentieth century, the control of the Nile has been extended. The Aswan system has been enlarged several times, with additional barrages and canals constructed, culminating in the Aswan High Dam, inaugurated in January, 1971. The farmland of northern Egypt has been converted from the ancient basin agriculture dependent upon natural seasonal flooding and the deposit of river-borne silt to perennial irrigation and the use of fertilizer. For the first time in history, there is no flow of silt into the Nile Delta.

As a result, Egypt has become the classic case of the complex of interrelated problems that can result from this degree of intervention into nature's hydrologic cycle. Egypt now faces growing problems of salinity and waterlogging due to perennial irrigation. Also, downstream, where the river's flow has been slowed, salty waters from the Mediterranean Sea are flooding the Nile Delta, covering thousands of acres of fertile farmland. Migrational paths of fish have been disturbed, and feeding grounds are being altered by the loss of nutrients that formerly flowed below the dam. The sardine fishery in the eastern Mediterranean has drastically declined in recent years. A reservoir some 300 miles long lies behind the giant fifth Aswan dam. Much water in this hot, dry area is lost locally through evaporation. Chemicals used to retard evaporation may be harmful to Lake Aswan fish that are being counted on to supply much-needed protein. And, surprisingly to the dam's planners, much more water than expected is escaping every year through the limestone lining the lake's bank. Because of excessive leakage, the reservoir may take two centuries to fill. Loss of the annual deposit of fertile silt on the floodplains is

*water and
bread*

giving rise to increasing use of fertilizer, with attendant problems of pollution. And the silt carried by the Nile is accumulating now in the reservoir instead. The hoped-for prosperity from the billion-dollar dam is jeopardized by the adverse side effects of ecological intervention of this magnitude. It is threatened also by Egypt's continuing rapid population growth.

One of the most costly and tragic side effects of the spread of modern irrigation in Egypt and in the river valleys of other parts of Africa, Asia, and northeastern South America is the great increase in the incidence of schistosomiasis. This debilitating intestinal and urinary disease is produced by the parasitic larva of a blood fluke that burrows into the flesh of a person standing in water-soaked fields. Aquatic snails that carry this schistosomiasis-producing fluke are invading reservoirs and irrigation canals. Fifty percent of the Egyptian people have the infection, and one out of ten deaths in Egypt is caused by it. The Chinese call this disease "snail fever" and are waging an all-out campaign against it. But schistosomiasis might also be called the poor man's emphysema because, like that disease, it is environmentally induced through conditions created by man. The snails and flukes thrive in perennial irrigation systems, where they come in close proximity to large human populations. Infected humans spread the microscopic larvae simply by bathing or urinating in streams and canals. The incidence of the disease is rising rapidly as the world's large rivers are harnessed for irrigation. Today schistosomiasis is estimated to afflict 250 million people, or one out of fourteen people living today. It surpasses malaria, the incidence of which is declining, as the world's most prevalent infectious disease.

The growing demand for food is forcing man to intervene more and more in the hydrologic cycle to develop water resources and is resulting in conflicts within nations, such as that existing among the states of California, Nevada, Arizona, New Mexico, and Colorado for rights to Colorado River waters. Water's immense value is also contributing to political conflict between nations, for example, between India and

Pakistan for water in the Indus River system, between Israel and Jordan for Jordan River water, between the Sudan and the United Arab Republic for Nile River water, and between Mexico and the United States for water from the Colorado River. Projected increases in population requirements for daily bread will call for more and more water, forcing man to consider even more massive and complex interventions in the hydrologic cycle. The desalting of seawater for irrigation purposes represents a major departure from traditional practices. Even more far-reaching is a Soviet plan to reverse the flow of four rivers currently flowing northward and emptying into the Arctic Sea. These rivers would be diverted southward into the semi-arid lands of southern Russia, greatly expanding the irrigated area in the Soviet Union and better enabling the Soviet Union to reduce the need for imported cereals and to meet the demand of its people for better diets. Climatologists, however, are concerned that shutting off the flow of relatively warm water from these four rivers would cool the Arctic and have far-reaching implications not only for the climate of the Arctic but for the climatic system of the entire earth.

The growing competition for scarce water supplies among states and among contending uses in the western United States is forcing consideration of massive interventions in the earth's hydrologic cycle in North America. For example, a detailed engineering plan exists to divert the Yukon River and other major rivers in Alaska and the Canadian Northwest southward across Canada into the western United States in order to meet the growing thirst for water for both agricultural and industrial purposes. Such an effort would cost an estimated $100 billion.

Agriculture claims much more of the earth's water than industry or human usage does, but man's crops use only a small share of the total water used by the earth's plants, probably far less than agriculture's portion of vegetation-covered land. This is true partly because natural vegetation provides permanent coverage in many places; whereas crops are seasonal, covering the land only part of the year.

Yet with water becoming an increasingly crucial commodity

for food production, man will have to pay increasing attention to the efficiency with which crops, particularly cereals, use water. Rice, the staple food for half of mankind, is the most extravagant user of water. Wheat usually yields far more calories and proteins with a given amount of water than rice does. Under some circumstances, wheat can be produced with one-third the water needed for rice. Fortunately, new varieties of both wheat and rice are physiologically more efficient in using water than traditional varieties are.

Among the cereals, sorghum is the most efficient user of water. It responds well to intensive irrigation, and it also tolerates drought far better than rice, wheat, or corn. In the event of severe moisture stress, sorghum simply becomes dormant, resuming growth when moisture supplies are replenished. These characteristics, plus sorghum's high protein content, are helping to make it increasingly popular in tropical and subtropical countries as well as in the dry southern American Great Plains. Grain sorghum is a natural dry-season crop to combine successfully with wet-season rice in multiple cropping or year-round farming. With enough water and fertilizer, certain varieties of sorghum "tiller" after harvest; that is, they generate new stems and leaves to produce second and third crops of grain from the original planting.

summary

Water has played an enormous role in the rise and fall of civilizations throughout history. Water and the efficiency with which it is managed will determine to a greater and greater degree man's food supply and the fortunes and levels of living of large numbers of human beings in the future. Increasingly it is the lack of water rather than the lack of land that is limiting food production.

SUGGESTED READINGS

Adams, Robert M., "The Origin of Cities," *Scientific American*, September, 1960.

Addison, Herbert, *Land*, *Water and Food*, London: Chapman and Hall, 1961.

58

man and his environment: food

Borgstrom, Georg, *Too Many, A Study of Earth's Biological Limitations*, New York: Macmillan, 1969.

Brown, Lester R., *Seeds of Change*, New York: Praeger, 1970.

Clawson, Marion, Hans H. Landsberg, and Lyle T. Alexander, "Desalted Seawater for Agriculture: Is It Economic?" *Science*, June 6, 1969.

Jacobson, Thorkild, and Robert M. Adams, "Salt and Silt in Ancient Mesopotamian Agriculture," *Science*, November 21, 1958.

Sterling, Claire, "Aswan Dam Looses a Flood of Problems," *Life*, February 12, 1971.

5
Columbus's contribution to world agriculture

We are not accustomed to linking Columbus with world agriculture and with a major advance in the population-sustaining capacity of the earth, but his contribution, however unintended, was profound. When he sailed across the formidable Atlantic and arrived in the New World at the end of the fifteenth century, he bridged the gap between two agricultural systems that, over many millennia, had developed independently.

Among the strongest supporting evidence for the independent origins of agriculture in the Old World and the New World is the fact that the crops and animals domesticated in the two regions were very different. Thus, when Columbus established the link between the two worlds, he set in motion an exchange of crops and livestock that has continued into the present and that has vastly altered the global distribution of plant and animal species. Interestingly, some species found much better ecological niches in the world to which they were transported and introduced than in their areas of origin. As this exchange progressed, the earth's capacity to sustain human populations on all continents expanded enormously.

From a present-day perspective, the years around A.D. 1500 mark the time when Western civilization burst out of the confines of the European continent and reached across the seas to every corner of the globe. Revolutionary changes took place in world relationships after Columbus and other European sailors opened the sea routes to distant continents. The Atlantic coast of Europe was no longer just the westernmost frontier of the Eurasian land mass. It quickly became the crossroads of newly forged worldwide sea lanes.

Along these sea lanes, European colonizers carried their crops to the New World, and their livestock and farming practices as well. The Europeans, however, found not only hunters in the Americas but also tillers who, despite some primitive farming methods, had much to give to world agriculture in the form of domesticated plants and agricultural techniques.

At the time Columbus arrived, agriculture in America was in many respects more primitive than in Europe because it lacked draft animals and the plow. And neither the wheel nor metal was in use in the New World. All agriculture was carried out by hand, using tools of wood or of stone, bone, or shell.

Indian agriculture in much of America resembled the more primitive agriculture found today in parts of sub-Saharan Africa, the hill and mountain regions of Southeast Asia, the outer islands of Indonesia, the Philippines, and northeastern Brazil. In the absence of saws or axes, forest area was cleared of natural cover to make fields by girdling trees or scorching their roots. As trees died, the land became exposed to sunlight and crops were planted. Dead trees and stumps were eventually burned, and their ashes, rich in potash, were used to replenish the soil. Many large clearings on fertile land were of great value to the first European settlers. As fields declined in fertility, the Indians shifted cultivation by clearing new land or by returning to previously cultivated fields that had been fallowed and rested for several years.

Europeans, in contrast, had learned to use land more intensively as population grew. They had developed several methods of rotating crops rather than land as a means of renewing the soil. They also used plows and draft animals. Livestock and crop production were closely interrelated in the European system. Livestock contributed animal power, food, and manure for fertilizing fields and gardens.

But even in the absence of tools and animal power known in the Old World, many agricultural arts in pre-Columbian America were highly developed. Irrigated agriculture, for example, had supported flourishing populations in certain areas of the New World: in all the coastal valleys of Peru sometime after A.D. 500 and in the Peruvian Andes, in Central America, and in the North American Southwest somewhat later. In pre-Columbian days, the unique chinampa farming system, dating back almost 2,000 years, overcame problems of drainage and supported the Aztecs and other relatively dense farming populations in the Valley of Mexico. *Chinampas* are long, narrow pieces of fertile land usually surrounded on three sides by canals and supporting gardens. When properly maintained, chinampas are capable of producing several crops a year while remaining fertile without fallowing.

The distinguishing feature of pre-Columbian agriculture in both North and South America, however, was intertillage. Whatever was planted—whether corn, manioc, potatoes, melons, or beans—was placed by hand in mounds of dirt or in prepared ridges. Farmers then could and did till between rows and mounds. The Indians also fertilized with fish. These sophisticated styles of cultivation were highly suitable for New World crops, soils, and, climate; but they were unfamiliar to the early settlers, who knew only the broadcast method of seeding, in which seeds were scattered widely over the ground, a method appropriate for their small-grains cultivation. Not until the settlers adopted native crops and agricultural methods was their food supply assured in the New World. Squanto taught them in Plymouth, it may be remembered, and Kemps and Tassore in Jamestown. Various methods of intertillage are practiced today in both New and Old World agriculture, greatly contributing to the earth's food-producing capacity. Modern corn production in the United States, for example, is based on the development and elaboration of Indian cultivation techniques. Intertillage has also enormously enlarged agricultural productivity in Asia as a central element of the Japanese paddy system of rice production. With this method, rice seedlings are started in a protected seedbed and transplanted to the paddy by hand, where they are carefully set in rows to permit the use of hand cultivators.

crops

Maize, beans, and squashes or pumpkins had been the dominant crops of Central and North America since 5000 B.C. New World Indians had advanced the art of cultivating them to a high level. They were almost always planted together and formed a most remarkable symbiotic and ecologically sophisticated relationship. The corn plants grew tall and were first to take advantage of sunlight and moisture. Beans claimed a share of sunlight by climbing up the corn stalks. Being legumes, they enriched the soil through colonies of nitrogen-fixing bacteria supported by their roots. It was not until later that soil-enriching leguminous crops such as alfalfa and clover were used widely in Europe in rotation with the customary cereal staples. While bean plants enriched the soil in New World fields, squash or pumpkin plants reached out over the ground, preventing excessive weed growth. Where the growing season was short, all three could be planted at the same time, since the corn was a variety that matured early. Where the growing season was long, corn was often planted first, and the beans and squash or pumpkin planted in the corn hill later. Growing mixed crops probably also reduced losses from diseases and insect depredations. Through millennia of selection, the Indian farmers developed varieties of corn that could be grown in highly diverse New and Old World environments. Through selecting and favoring, they also developed beans that were high in protein and oil and suited to virtually all climates and soils. They were so superior to Old World pulses that they rapidly became important additions to Old World gardens from western Europe to China and Japan, improving diets wherever they spread.

From pre-Columbian domestication, world agriculture has

63

also inherited avocados, cashews, agaves, chili peppers, sunflowers, tomatoes, Jerusalem artichokes, cocoa, cassava or manioc, papaya, pineapples, cotton (*Gossypium hirsutum* L.), white potatoes, sweet potatoes, peanuts, and tobacco. Peru and Bolivia, the highlands of Mexico and Guatemala, and perhaps the Amazon basin were the great centers of original cultivation in the Americas. Apparently only the Jerusalem artichoke, sunflower, and several plum and grape species were first tamed in what is now the United States. The Indians also gathered and ate many nuts and fruits that have since been domesticated: chestnuts, pecans, black walnuts, hazelnuts, blackberries, blueberries, crabapples, cranberries, dewberries, elderberries, grapes, huckleberries, plums, raspberries, and strawberries.

Crops first domesticated by the Indians accounted for nearly half the U.S. crop output, measured at farm value, during the early 1960s. Corn, or Indian maize, is the most important indigenous crop. It was probably first domesticated in Central America shortly before 5000 B.C. and played an important role in the development of pre-Columbian Indian civilizations. Today the annual crop in the United States exceeds that of all other grains combined. The major U.S. cotton variety (*Gossypium hirsutum* L.), first grown by the Indians of Mexico, is today the mainstay of the world's cotton crop. Tobacco, white potatoes, and peanuts are other Indian crops that play important roles in contemporary American agriculture.

Many crops not among the indigenous plants listed above now cover huge stretches of land in the New World. The New World affords a good illustration of the way in which introducing non-native crops has greatly augmented the food-producing capacity of the land. Wheat, barley, rye, and oats were carried in Spanish, French, and English ships from the Old World to the New along the sea lanes opened by Columbus and others. Wheat and barley were domesticated before 7000 B.C. in southwestern Asia, where they originated. They were taken into Europe by early Neolithic colonizers and were being cultivated in England before 2000 B.C. Oats and rye, accidentally carried to Europe as weeds mixed in with wheat and barley, proved adaptable to ecological conditions there and were domesticated.

In the New World, the environment was highly favorable for the small grains (wheat, rye, barley, and oats). And interestingly enough, without them, much of the vast land area of the lower-rainfall region in the United States and other areas of the New World would have remained in grass, for corn requires more moisture than is commonly available over a large part of the Great Plains and elsewhere. Wheat eventually replaced corn as the staple New World food, and corn became the principal feed grain. American wheat has fed tens of millions outside North America during recent years. And Mexican wheat, in extraordinary modern varieties, is now revolutionizing agriculture in many parts of the world, including its ancient homeland in the Middle East (see Chapter 10).

Other crops were brought from the Old World to the New by early European sailors and settlers: alfalfa, flax, sugarcane, apricots, European grapes, lemons, olives, oranges, peaches, pears, walnuts, hemp, and indigo.

Most of the leading crops produced on U.S. farms today were either domesticated by the Indians or introduced from Europe. But there are some significant exceptions. The principal source of vegetable oil in the United States and the leading U.S. farm export today is the soybean, a crop introduced from China several decades ago. Mainland China was the world's major soybean producer a generation ago, supplying around 90 percent of all soybeans entering the world market. China's expanding population has diminished the outflow to a trickle in recent years. Today the United States produces three-fourths of the world soybean crop and provides some 90 percent of the soybeans in the international marketplace. Soybeans became important in North America and Europe during World War II as a substitute for other protein foods and as a source of oil. Today they are valued as food, livestock feed, and industrial raw material. But beyond that, as legumes they enrich the soil by fixing atmospheric nitrogen and are therefore a desirable crop to be planted in rotation with other crops such as corn.

Grain sorghum, now the second-ranking feed grain in the United States (after corn), was brought across the Atlantic from Africa with the early slaves. Sorghum constituted the food stores on board many slave ships during the long ocean crossing along the Middle Passage. In the New World, many slaves continued to grow small patches of sorghum for food. But until the Great Plains were settled, the value of sorghum was not fully realized. Sorghum is drought-resistant, and turned out to be remarkably well adapted to the semi-arid low-rainfall areas of many western states. Sorghum has been increasingly accepted as a feed grain both in the United States and elsewhere. Today the United States is the world's leading producer and exporter of grain sorghum.

After Columbus, many New World crops moved across the seas to affect the population-sustaining capacity of the earth elsewhere. The introduction of the New World potato into northwestern Europe and China greatly augmented the food supply, permitting marked increases in population. This is most dramatically illustrated in the case of Ireland, where the population increased rapidly for several decades on the strength of the expanded food supply that the potato made available. Only when the blight *Phytophtora infestans* devastated the potato crop in 1846 was population checked in Ireland. The potato became almost as common in northern Europe as rice is in southeast Asia. During the two world wars of this century, the potato sustained the German people.

Rubber, the crop that eventually put the world on wheels, was indigenous to the Amazon Basin. Today Asia produces approximately 90 percent of the world's natural rubber. Rubber plants were taken from South America to Asia by the British via the Royal Botanical Gardens.

Corn, the only cereal crop indigenous to the New World, is now produced on every continent. It is the only one of the three principal grains (wheat, rice, and corn) to be widely used as both a food and a feed grain. It has become a leading feed grain in many countries and a dietary staple in others. In the northern part of the Western Hemisphere, corn is largely a feed grain. But in Latin America, it is a food staple. In Africa and Asia, most of the corn produced is consumed as food. In Thailand, the emergence of corn as an important factor in the economy has been exceptional; exports of corn now exceed those of rice. Corn is the principal staple in Kenya, where more is consumed per person than in any New World country.

The principal source of vegetable oil in the Soviet Union is the sunflower, a crop that was domesticated by pre-Columbian Indians and that still grows wild in the Great Plains area of the United States. Cassava, or manioc, was taken by the Portuguese from Brazil to Africa in the 1600s, where it has become a dominant crop in subsistence agriculture in the sub-Saharan region. The cultivation of cassava greatly enlarged the population-sustaining capacity of sub-Saharan Africa. Strawberries, another crop indigenous to the New World, have proven popular everywhere.

livestock

Thus, the exchange of crops between the New World and the Old has been very much a two-way exchange; but this was not originally the case with livestock. There were no cattle, horses, or hogs in the New World when Columbus arrived. The New World is indebted to the Old for all its livestock and, with the exception of the turkey and muscovy duck, for all its poultry. The Incas did domesticate the llama and alpaca for use in haulage and the guinea pig for food and use in ceremonies. But the husbanding of these animals remained local and did not spread to other parts of the world, with the possible exception of the guinea pig, which was also raised in the Carribbean region. The earliest horses lived 40–50 million years ago in the New World, mainly in the region that is now the Great Plains. Similar animals existed then in the Old World, but became extinct. The New World species migrated across land bridges to Eurasia, becoming the ancestors of domesticated Old World horses. Horses were never domesticated in the New World;

they mysteriously became extinct, probably around the time that man first arrived there, 30,000–50,000 years ago. Stone Age men in the Old World hunted horses for food. But eventually man was to use horses more for transport and draft.

Herd animals (sheep, goats, cattle, and swine) were domesticated in southwestern Asia; donkeys, in Africa; and horses, in Central Asia. Water buffaloes, zebus or humped cattle, and chickens seem to have been domesticated on the Indo-Pakistan subcontinent; domesticated geese, pigs, and ducks (except the muscovy) probably originated in southeastern Asia.

Early settlers brought cattle, horses, pigs, sheep, goats, chickens, and ducks to the Americas. Throughout the early settlement period, farmers were too busy clearing new land and pushing the frontier westward to be intensively concerned with selective breeding. But in the nineteenth century, as agriculture became well established and the frontier receded westward, attention turned to improving farm animals for food and draft. In order to improve stock, it was necessary to turn to Europe for high-quality purebred animals. Today, however, American livestock are sold all over the world as breeding animals. Remarkable progress in genetics and breeding have made America the leading international source of breeding cattle and poultry.

summary

The movement of crops and animals between the two worlds, among continents and countries, continues as man alters the nature of the crops themselves through genetic manipulation, as he alters the environment, and as these two factors interact with the changing demands of the marketplace. During the centuries between the linking of Old and New Worlds at the end of the fifteenth and the modern agricultural revolution in the twentieth, some of the most dynamic advances in world agriculture and in the population-sustaining capacity of the globe sprang from the exchange of crops that was set in motion by Columbus.

*man and his
environment:
food*

SUGGESTED READINGS

Coe, Michael D., "The Chinampas of Mexico," *Scientific American*, July, 1964.

Sauer, Carl O., *Agricultural Origins and Dispersals*, Cambridge, Mass.: M.I.T. Press, 1969.

Zeuner, Frederick Eberhard, *A History of Domesticated Animals*, New York: Harper & Row, 1963.

6
harnessing energy for agriculture

For the first several thousand years (perhaps 5,000 or more) that man practiced agriculture, he relied entirely upon his own energies and muscle power for tilling, planting, and harvesting his farm fields. In New World agriculture, this was still the modus operandi when Columbus arrived at the end of the fifteenth century, roughly 8½ millennia after the earliest known cultivation of plants in the Western Hemisphere.

Harnessing the energies of draft animals was a major agricultural breakthrough. Draft animals were probably first used for transporting men and goods, and it was known that men were riding horses in the area near the Persian Gulf before 3500 B.C. Just where and when man first hitched primitive plows to cattle (first domesticated in southwestern Asia around 5000 B.C.) or horses (domesticated somewhat later in Central Asia), it is not possible to say. The breakthrough came later than the discovery of irrigation, but it was early nevertheless. It is certain that sometime before 3000 B.C., farmers of the Middle East had learned to harness draft animals to help them till the soil.

The use of animals much stronger than himself as a source of power greatly augmented man's own limited muscle power. Because most draft animals are ruminants, they are able to obtain a large part of their nourishment from roughage (such as grass, clover, alfalfa, hay, and straw) that is inedible to man. This provided man with a way of converting roughage into a usable form of energy and thus freed him to use some of his own energy for pursuits other than the quest for food. Strictly speaking, horses are nonruminants, but they can eat roughage as ruminants because of exceptional digestive systems. With animal power, around 10 percent of the population was freed from the land for other pursuits.

Oxen and horses have been the major draft animals used by man for farm work. Throughout antiquity, oxen were the primary draft animals used in agriculture, and they remain so in many parts of the world today. *Oxen* is a general term that most commonly designates castrated bulls used for draft purposes; it includes Middle Eastern and European cattle, zebus (or humped cattle), yaks, and water buffaloes. Oxen are called *bullocks* in many parts of Asia, especially on the Indo-Pakistan subcontinent. Both the docility and strength of the ox, or bullock, made him valuable to man in tilling the land. Cattle and zebus became widely used in wheat-growing areas of Europe and Asia that lie north of the wheat–rice line which stretches across Asia from just north of Bombay to Shanghai. Water buffaloes became associated with rice areas south of the line, since they had greater tolerance than cattle for hot, wet growing conditions. In the Nile valley, also, water buffaloes came to be used for tillage. In Tibet and other high Asian areas, yaks served more often as beasts of burden for transporting goods, as did llamas and alpacas of the high Andes; thin oxygen at high altitudes made movement stressful and inhibited the utilization of these animals for riding and for plowing fields. Camels, too, have been used in tilling fields, particularly in western India, but probably only in more recent history. Horses were valued in antiquity mainly for speed and were used for transport rather than for habitual plowing.

Early animal-drawn implements were crude, little more than pointed sticks; but they were adequate to free the dry, light soils of much of the Middle East, Asia, and the Mediterranean area. And hitches were inefficient. Plows were often hitched directly to the horns of an ox or to a simple form of yoke or collar laid across the neck, as pictured in Sumerian or Egyptian art. This method of hitching placed great strain on the animal's neck, preventing him from throwing the weight of his body into his work. Under such conditions, only a fraction of the muscle power of draft animals could be secured for the work at hand. The harnessing of horses was even more inadequate because the collar was set high on the throat instead of resting on the shoulder blades and the plow was attached on the back of the horse's neck. The collar tended to press against the horse's windpipe, choking him as he pulled forward. And the high point of traction prevented the horse from throwing his body forward. When points of traction are low, just above the shoulders on each side of the body, tractive efforts tend to hold the collar in place against the shoulder blades, thus interfering minimally with the animal's efforts to throw his weight into work.

The full utilization of animal power in antiquity was further impeded by inadequate foot protection. What foot protection there was for oxen and horses, in the form of leather or iron sandals bound to hoofs by thongs, was used in curing foot problems rather than in systematically protecting the feet of draft animals. Man's inability to harness more than one pair of animals was still another limitation on the use of power in the field. Techniques of harnessing and shoeing remained crude and inefficient throughout classical times.

Improvements in subsequent centuries in harnessing single animals, pairs of animals, and multiple teams in tandem, as well as in shoeing and in the plow, greatly increased the contribution that draft power made to the production of food. An efficient harness appeared in China under the Han dynasty in the fourth century B.C., when a rigid collar that rested on the animal's shoulders was developed. It was not used in Europe and western Asia until centuries later, however. The iron horseshoe with nails took hold in Europe and Asia around A.D. 900. Without horseshoes, a draft animal working on hard ground wore its feet out rapidly, and a small foot injury could easily disable an otherwise healthy animal. Both horses and oxen became much more efficient and durable when they were regularly clad in iron shoes. The plow, too, had undergone major improvement. By the twelfth century, the new devices had been firmly and widely adopted, and man's food-producing capacity had correspondingly expanded, particularly because these advances, combined with the development of communal farming, made possible the opening of vast new areas of rich, heavy, wet soil such as that found in northern Europe.

With more efficient harnessing and shoeing, horses, working perhaps twice as fast as oxen, were employed more and more in farm labor in northern Europe, where climatic conditions and reduced fallowing of land made possible a surplus of oats for feeding horses. In time, horses supplanted oxen in farm work in northern Europe and North America.

It has been conservatively estimated that draft animals in antiquity could accomplish only one-third of what heavier and more efficiently harnessed nineteenth- and twentieth-century animals could. Even so, an average draft animal in ancient times could perform around ten times as much work in a day as an average man.

Draft animals, primarily oxen and camels, have also been used for nonfield farming operations such as threshing grain and turning wheels to raise water for irrigation, particularly throughout Asia and Africa. From the time that man originally harnessed draft energy until he harnessed fossil-fuel energy for agriculture, the only other sources of power tapped for agriculture were wind and water. But these were applied to farming only to a very limited degree, and their use was confined to nonfield operations, such as threshing and delivering irrigation water, in specific geographical areas.

mechanical power

Some 5,000 years after the harnessing of draft animals, man developed the internal-combustion machine and the farm tractor, thus augmenting his own energies and those of his draft animals with mechanical power based on fossil fuels. This was a tremendous breakthrough, giving man a quantum jump in the amount of per capita energy available for agricultural work. Fossil fuels gave man other advantages as well: They were mobile, storable, and adaptable to various farm operations.

It has been roughly estimated that most agricultural societies prior to the Industrial Revolution had, in general, an overall per capita energy consumption below 15,000 calories per day, perhaps less than 10,000, most of which was used for producing food and keeping warm. In many agricultural societies, slavery was one consequence of this general scarcity of other forms of available energy. Low per capita energy in traditional agriculture, depending almost entirely on raw manpower and animal power, tied at least four-fifths of a society's population to the land. Efficient harnessing of modern energy sources has permitted the productivity of agricultural labor to multiply ten, twenty, or thirty times. Fossil fuels have provided most of this additional energy. With mechanical power based on fossil fuels, it has become possible in the twentieth century for a small minority (less than 5 percent in the United States, for example) to feed an entire population.

Fossil fuels are a form of stored energy resulting from past photosynthesis. Tapping them enabled man to substitute the product of eons-old photosynthesis—petroleum—for that of present photosynthesis—the oats, corn, and hay grown as feed for draft animals. For example, the replacement of horses by tractors in the United States not only provided farmers with several times as much power but also released 70 million acres of farmland, formerly devoted to feeding horses, for the raising of food crops and for other purposes. In intensively mechanized Taiwan, an estimated 80,000 hectares of land would be required to feed the draft animals needed for tilling the current cultivated area. One might guess that acreage around the world freed by substituting tractors for horses and other draft animals easily amounts to a quarter of a billion acres.

To sum up, then, man's increasing capacity to harness the energy supply of the earth's ecosystem has enabled him to pursue the quest for more food using three levels of energy input: (1) manpower alone; (2) manpower plus animal power;

and (3) manpower plus mechanical power based mainly on fossil fuels. Today most farmers in Nepal, as well as in other scattered areas throughout Asia, Latin America, and Africa, rely on manpower alone. Use of draft animals is still widespread. Close to half of the planet's farmland may currently be plowed by draft animals rather than tractors. In Colombia today one finds all three forms widely applied: large commercial farmers use tractors; small farmers use draft power; and Indians in the highlands eke out subsistence livings with the meager energy inputs of farmer and family.

On a global basis, the available horsepower (hp) per hectare of arable land and land under permanent crop is 0.36. This is an assessment of the power available for field work based on numbers of farm workers, draft animals, and tractors. The distribution of this energy among manpower, draft power, and mechanical power is as follows: Man provides only 0.024 hp, or around 7 percent of the total; animals, 0.044, or around 12 percent; and tractors, 0.290, or around 80 percent.

The amount of energy expended per hectare and yields per hectare are closely associated. Asia, with a yearly energy availability in agriculture of only 0.2 hp per hectare, has an average crop yield, principally grain, of 840 kilograms (kg) per hectare; the United States, with an energy availability of only 1 hp per hectare, achieves an average crop yield of 2,600 kg per hectare. The United Kingdom and Japan, both cultivating very intensively, use about 2 hp per hectare and attain yields of more than 5,000 kg per hectare. At least 0.5 hp per hectare is needed to realize most of the production potential of farmland. Beyond that, additional energy apparently is used more to save labor and less to further raise yields. Recognition of the close relationship between energy supply and the productivity of cropland is quite recent.

The extent to which mechanical power has been substituted for human power and animal power in agriculture is evident in the large number of tractors in advanced regions such as North America, Oceania, and Europe: around 13 million tractors, or approximately 93 percent of the world total. And this is in spite of the greater area of farmland in Asia, Africa, and Latin

America. Almost a million four-wheel tractors are in use in the developing regions, and their numbers have been increasing at around 5–7 percent a year. In North America, tractors (numbering more than 5.4 million in 1966) have completely supplanted horses, except for their use by a few farmers such as the Mennonites.

Traditionally, particularly in Western nations, the use of mechanical power has been thought of in connection with saving labor. But mechanical power is also related in a number of ways to gaining higher yields. As agriculture has become more complex over time, this relationship has become more evident. For example, a man using a sprayer and foot-operated pump cannot distribute all pesticides with sufficient uniformity. Applying modern fungicides and other pesticides to crops evenly and effectively depends on power dusters and high-pressure sprayers. Mechanical power also contributes to more food by making possible better plowing and seedbed preparation; better timing of planting, harvesting, and threshing; and greater opportunity for multiple cropping, particularly by providing irrigation water and shortening crop cycles.

The use of mechanical power in agriculture progressed most rapidly in the United States, where a favorable man/land ratio spurred the process. The country was sparsely populated and relatively rich in resources; labor was scarce; holdings were large. Consequently, emphasis was on output per man rather than output per acre. Even before mechanical power, the United States had a history of labor-saving efforts. The invention of the horse-drawn reaper in the 1830s was the first of a long series of mechanical inventions designed for this purpose, including the grain drill, the mowing machine, the two-horse straddle cultivator, and many others. Early uses of mechanical power in agriculture during steam engine, pre-internal-combustion engine days were confined mainly to nonfield operations such as threshing. Because of their heaviness, steam engines were suited primarily for stationary operations. Grain was cut, put in sheaves, and taken to the farmyard to be processed by steam-driven threshers.

Tractors were the first application of mechanical power to

farm field work. Most of the transition in the United States from horses to tractors was made during a period of a few decades in the twentieth century, mainly between World War I and World War II. In 1920, there were only a few tractors on U.S. farms and around 25 million draft horses. Today there are almost 5 million tractors in the United States, or an average of 2 tractors per farm or 1 for every person in the agricultural labor force, and virtually no draft horses. However, the actual number of tractors in the United States may be declining because horsepower per tractor is rising and the number of people in farming is declining.

Self-propelled combines, coming into their own largely during the 1950s, make it possible today to harvest and thresh grain in one field operation. A combine manned by one farmer can harvest sixty-five acres a day. A corn harvester can reap and bag three acres of corn in an hour. The use of mechanical power has progressed to the point where American rice is planted and fertilized mostly by plane. And wheat is planted, cultivated, fertilized, harvested, and threshed almost entirely by mechanical power, and is not touched by human hands until it reaches the table.

The high cost of mechanization has given rise to a great amount of custom-hire work. Throughout the Great Plains, from Texas to Canada, most of the grain (mainly wheat, barley, and oats) is harvested by self-propelled combines. Two people, often father and son, equipped with a combine and two trucks, will begin in Texas in late May or early June in time to harvest the winter wheat crop. After cutting and threshing the grain, the combine unloads it with a blower into the truck, and then it is delivered to grain elevators. The team gradually moves northward, harvesting in Oklahoma, Kansas, Colorado, the Dakotas; reaching Montana in late September in time to harvest the spring wheat crop (planted in early spring and harvested in late fall); and then moving on to Canada to do the same thing.

In 1870, one American farmer could produce enough food to feed five people. Today, with the use of mechanical power in combination with other inputs, one farmer in the United States can feed forty-three people.

Japan, an agriculturally advanced nation with an unfavorable man/land ratio, has applied mechanical power more to raising yields than to saving labor. Japanese farmers, supplementing their own energy input of 0.15 hp per hectare per year with 0.09 hp from animals and 2.06 hp of mechanical power, for a total of 2.3 hp, use more energy per hectare in producing food than any other country, including the United States. The yields they attain are among the highest in the world.

The Japanese have adapted the internal-combustion engine to small farms by developing two-wheeled power tillers commonly called *garden tractors*. More than 2.5 million garden tractors were being used in Japan in 1965, a fivefold increase from 1960. The draft-animal stage of energy input was essentially bypassed in Japan because the pressure of population necessitated using scarce land to raise food for man.

On today's farms, various nonfield operations are being powered by inanimate energy sources other than fossil fuels. Hydroelectric power is being used for pumping water, milking cows, grinding and mixing feed, heating and lighting poultry houses, incubating eggs. Most of the 16 million dairy cows in the United States are being milked by electric power. In some areas, nuclear energy is supplying agriculture with electric power, but only to a limited degree thus far. In several poor countries (India, for example), the new and exciting spread of small-scale irrigation using electric pumps and tubewells is associated with the spread of rural electrification.

The major share of the power available in Asia, Africa, and Latin America is human and animal power. Even animal-drawn moldboard plows are hardly used in these regions. Instead, the centuries-old wooden plow is used. Farmers in India, where yields are still among the world's lowest, use only about one-fourth horsepower per hectare. Less than one-tenth horsepower comes from mechanical power.

The key to intensification of agriculture in a large part of the tropical–subtropical world is a substantial increase in the amount of water used for irrigation. In many situations, this can be achieved only with the use of mechanical pumps and diesel or electric engines.

Dependence on either human or animal power to pump water imposes serious constraints on the amount of water that can be available for irrigation. A study of pumping costs in India indicates that it costs 495 rupees to pump 10 acre-inches of water by hand, assuming a 40-ft lift. With animal power, using a Persian wheel, the cost drops to 345 rupees, but the really startling gain comes with the use of a diesel engine, when the cost drops to 60 rupees. The cost advantages of mechanizing irrigation pumping are perhaps greater than in any other agricultural operation. This helps to explain why the use of mechanical power for irrigation is increasing so rapidly in the developing countries.

Results from a growing body of research on the economics of farm mechanization in the developing countries indicate that many farm operations, especially seedbed preparation, can be performed much more economically with tractors than with draft animals.

New technologies are bringing with them new requirements for mechanization. The use of pesticides, now becoming essential because of the heavy capital outlays involved in the recently developed high-yielding varieties, sometimes requires high-pressure sprayers. Early maturing rice varieties that ripen during the monsoon pose special problems in drying. Mechanical grain drying must replace the age-old method of sun drying.

One of the constraints on mechanization in the developing countries is the small size of land holdings with their still smaller fields. Small farmers often simply cannot afford the capital investment required to purchase even a small tractor. If these farmers are to benefit from the advantages of mechanization, they must have access to custom-hire services. In some countries such as Thailand, where farmers maintain a team of water buffaloes solely for preparing the rice seedbed once each year, the possibility of hiring someone with a tractor to plow the rice fields means these farmers can dispense with their buffaloes, incurring substantial savings in the process. Prior to the availability of custom plowing, there was little choice but to maintain a team of buffaloes.

Some farmers in India, whose holdings are actually much smaller than the optimum size for one team of bullocks, pay a very high price for the limited amount of use they make of their bullock team. Again, with the availability of custom-hiring tractor service, they may be able to dispense with their bullock teams at a substantial saving. The creation of custom-hire services is one of the most effective ways of bridging the gap between the economies of scale of farm equipment and the size of farms common to many of the more densely populated countries.

It should be remembered that agriculture really fathered the Industrial Revolution. And then, in turn, the Industrial Revolution, with the harnessing of new sources of energy at its center, fathered the modern agricultural revolution. But the revolution in industrial production and technology that began 200 years ago, spawning first the steam engine and later the internal-combustion machine, contributed more to agriculture than merely the harnessing of fossil-fuel energy for cultivating fields and performing other farm operations. With the development and expansion of a vast store of new technologies and of the industrial and service sectors of modern societies, agriculture gained an enormous array of resources, resources essential to keep food production in line with mankind's expanding food needs.

As long as there is an abundance of new land to bring under the plow, continuing population growth does not pose any serious problem for traditional agriculture. The frontier is simply pushed back a bit farther. Land and labor, the key inputs, are readily available. Seed and draft animals, the principal capital inputs, are self-generated on the farm. Next year's seed is saved from this year's crop. Technology does not greatly change. Inputs are not needed from the rest of the economy.

Modern chemically oriented and often mechanized agriculture, however, which has been spreading through the world during the twentieth century as frontiers have disappeared, not only depends heavily on more energy input applied directly to the farm field but also uses large amounts of purchased inputs to raise the productivity of land. In countries where there is no new land to plow, agricultural growth is entirely dependent on the rest of the economy for the goods and service needed to generate and sustain a takeoff in yield per acre. Fertilizers, pesticides, implements, improved plant varieties, and a wide array of other inputs are needed. All must come from the nonfarm sector. Required services, such as research, credit, transportation and marketing facilities, and know-how, are as essential as the physical inputs themselves.

The extent to which modern farmers depend upon the non-agricultural sector for inputs to "make two blades of grass grow where one once grew" underlines the contribution of the Industrial Revolution to agriculture. Consider, for example, the variety and scale of purchased inputs in the United States, whose agriculture fed 200 million Americans and 100 million people elsewhere during the 1960s. The farm inputs purchased by U.S. farmers totaled $21.5 billion in 1965. Approximately $9 billion of this represented feed and livestock purchases, many of them from other farmers. The remaining $12.5 billion of purchased inputs came from outside the farm sector. Included among the wide variety of inputs used were petroleum products ($1.5 billion), fertilizer and lime ($1.7 billion), and equipment parts and repairs ($525 million). A sampling of other items includes electricity, all kinds of containers, twine for binding hay bales, veterinary services, and animal antibiotics. The complete list of purchased inputs is pages long. For each of the 300 million acres cultivated, American farmers spend $42 annually on production requisites supplied by the nonfarm sector.

Although farms in the United States are quite large on the average, greater agricultural output from the intensive use of inputs is not confined to a system of large holdings. Japan and Taiwan, with farms averaging only 2.5 and 3.1 acres, respectively, have two of the world's most advanced farm sectors. Japan's farmers, with a high-rainfall rice culture and a more intensive mode of cultivation, spend even more per acre than do their American counterparts. Their per-acre expenditures for agricultural chemicals alone—fertilizer, insecticides, fungicides, and herbicides—now exceed per-acre expenditures for all production requisites in the United States. In addition, although Japanese farmers typically operate on a small scale, each year they spend more than five dollars an acre for farm implements and power equipment. This is almost exactly the same expenditure per acre as in the United States. Whereas U.S. farmers buy one tractor for, say, 150 acres, Japanese farmers buy a number of small garden-type tillers for the same area.

Most of the know-how and wherewithal for modern agriculture has been developed and produced by large industrial firms of North America, Europe, and Japan and distributed to farmers in these regions. Only in the last few years have these resources begun to cross national boundaries to the poor countries on a scale and in a manner sufficient to significantly affect agricultural production.

summary

Agriculture remains a major consumer of energy in both agricultural and industrial societies. In the poor countries, the greater part of the energy supply, most of which is human and animal power, is used to produce food. As countries develop, the quantity of energy consumed in the farm sector increases even though the agricultural share of total energy consumption declines.

Where agriculture is highly mechanized today, the expenditure of fossil-fuel energy per acre is often substantially greater than the energy produced on the acre, that is, the energy embodied in food. This deficit in output is of no immediate consequence as long as man can draw on energy in the bank, that is, the energy stored in subterranean fossil-fuel deposits, to supplement the current influx of solar energy.

For the present and for the purposes of agriculture alone, the energy budget of the earth's ecosystem is still favorable. The supply of solar energy, both the energy stored in fossil fuels and that being captured daily and converted into food energy by crops, enables an advanced nation to be fed with only 5 percent of the population employed directly in agriculture.

Since world production of petroleum is expected to peak within the foreseeable future (perhaps around the turn of the century according to M. King Hubbert), man will eventually either have to return to the more traditional forms of agriculture, relying on his own energies and those of draft animals, or turn to some other source of motive energy for agriculture, perhaps nuclear energy or some means, other than photosynthesis, of harnessing solar energy. Harnessing large power supplies directly from solar energy appears, to date, to be technologically unpromising. Very little nuclear energy is used at present to produce food except in the few areas where nuclear-based power-generating plants provide electricity for farm use. Cows, for instance, are being milked and poultry houses are being heated with nuclear energy. But thus far, no field-tillage operations are fueled by nuclear energy, since there is not yet an efficient means of converting it into a more mobile form. This may eventually be forthcoming, since man is currently powering submarines and ships with nuclear energy, and since nuclear-powered rockets are on the drawing boards or perhaps already at the test stage.

SUGGESTED READINGS

Cippola, Carol M., *The Economic History of World Population*, Baltimore: Penguin, 1964.

Food and Agriculture Organization of the United Nations, *The State of Food and Agriculture 1968*, Rome: FAO, 1968.

Giles, G. W., "Agricultural Power and Equipment," in President's Science Advisory Committee, *The World Food Problem*, Report of the Panel on the World Food Supply, vol. 3, Washington, D. C.: U.S. Government Printing Office, 1963.

Hubbert, M. King, "Energy Resources," in *Resources and Man*, Committee on Resources and Man, National Academy of Sciences–National Research Council, San Francisco: W. H. Freeman, 1969.

harnessing energy for agriculture

Kranzberg, Melvin, and Carroll W. Pursell, Jr., eds., *Technology in Western Civilization*, New York: Oxford University Press, 1967.

Odum, Howard T., "Energetics of World Food Production," in President's Science Advisory Committee, *The World Food Problem*, Report of the Panel on the World Food Supply, vol. 3, Washington, D. C.: U. S. Government Printing Office, 1963.

Usher, Abbott Payson, *A History of Mechanical Inventions*, Boston: Beacon Press, 1959.

Fussell, G. E., *Farming Technique from Prehistoric to Modern Times*, London: Pergamon Press Ltd., 1965.

7
the
ocean
as a
source
of food

Faced with the buildup of population pressure on the land in recent history, man has been looking with quickening interest to the ocean as a source of food, particularly protein. Japan, the first nation to systematically move in this direction, is perhaps the best specific illustration. Japan was forced to turn to the ocean for protein almost a century ago in order to concentrate on using its land for cultivating rice. The typical Japanese fish and rice diet has its roots in the population–land crisis of the last decades of the nineteenth century, when Japan was already a virtually fixed-land economy with a growing population. Today, Japan, dependent on the sea for around 60 percent of its animal protein intake, is the world's second-ranking fishing nation, capturing more than 12 percent of the total catch. With a population of 100 million people squeezed into a mountainous land area smaller than California, Japan must use nearly all its scarce arable land to meet food-energy needs.

Men through the centuries have tended to regard the enormous ocean as a reservoir of vast, inexhaustible food resources. T. H. Huxley

reflected this view in his inaugural address at the International
Fisheries Exhibition in London in 1883.

*I believe that it may be affirmed with confidence that, in
relation to our present mode of fishing, a number of the
most important sea fisheries such as the cod fishery, the
herring fishery and the mackerel fishery are inexhaustible.
And, I base this conviction on two grounds: first, that the
number we catch is relatively insignificant; and secondly,
that the magnitude of the destructive agencies at work upon
them is so prodigious, that the destruction effected by the
fisherman cannot seriously increase the death rate. . . .* [*]

But modern man has extended his intervention in the ocean
far more than earlier man, with the exception of the Jules
Vernes, would have dreamed. Both the scale of fishing and
fishing techniques have changed phenomenally in the twentieth century, particularly since World War II. Consequently
the number of fish caught, which has multiplied tenfold in the
past 100 years, is no longer insignificant relative to the number
produced annually in the sea. The press of man on the world's
fishing grounds is one of the less-visible but increasingly important dramas of modern times. Furthermore, man has introduced a new destructive agency in the form of oceanic pollution, with consequences for aquatic plant and fish life that are
just beginning to be known.

Fishing fleets of some nations such as the Soviet Union and
Japan have grown to giant size during the unprecedented and
sensational postwar effort to mobilize the fish resources of the
seas. The Soviet Union has developed floating fishing cities
that accommodate 10,000–30,000 men and women and include transport vessels, mother ships, freezer trawlers, and
large factory ships—virtually independent industrial units.
Processing facilities for freezing, salting, canning, and manufac-

---

[*]Quoted in B. B. Parrish, "Obtaining the Maximum Yield from Traditional Methods of Harvesting," in J. D. Ovington, ed., *The Better Use of
the World's Fauna for Food* (London: Institute of Biology, 1963),
p. 79.

turing fishmeal make it possible to preserve the fish on the spot. The Japanese pattern has been to establish bilateral arrangements with nations around the world for processing facilities on land near fishing grounds.

These modern fishing fleets are highly mobile and range widely over the oceans. Soviet fishing fleets are at work on all the world's major fishing banks—in the Atlantic, Pacific, and Indian oceans and in the Mediterranean and Black seas. The Japanese are also fishing in all oceans and as far away from their shore as Greenland and Iceland. Several East European countries, including Yugoslavia, Romania, Bulgaria, Poland, and East Germany (wealthier countries that, together with the Soviet Union, have an abnormally high dependence on starchy staples like potatoes and want to increase their protein supply), are creating long-distance fishing fleets equipped with processing facilities.

Traditionally fish have been located by sight and by trial fishing for fish swimming deeper. Today visual detection is aided by space-age aerial scouting. For example, ship-based helicopters in the whaling industry search for whales and communicate their findings to the whaling boats. Many commercial fisheries, including the whaling and herring industries, are using sonar equipment to locate submerged fish. Japanese tuna long-liners, roaming the seven seas, use temperature measurements to find tuna concentrations. Methods of catching fish have also advanced with the use of lights and electrodes to attract fish and with improved nets and pumps to land them. The future will bring even more sophisticated technological advances in detecting, catching, and processing fish. For example, orbiting satellites, using aerial photography, will be able to locate fish-rich areas around the world, such as deep blue coastal upwelling areas that bring up nutrients from the ocean floor.

With an all-out hunt for the ocean's protein underway, it is no wonder that newspapers are sprinkled almost daily with accounts of disputes resulting from fishing ships of one nation penetrating the territorial waters of another. Japanese vessels

are no longer welcome in waters near China and have antago-
nized Mexico by their exploits. Russian fishing ships are repeat-
edly entering the coastal waters of Canada, the United States,
and Latin America. Peru and other Latin American countries
have seized more than a hundred U.S. fishing boats in the past
decade in disputes over the limits of territorial waters.

Man's intensified fishing efforts since World War II have
tripled fish production, a greater increase than that of any
other major food commodity. The world fish catch reached 64
million tons in 1968, compared with a grain harvest of almost
1 billion tons. Around 12 million tons of the catch was
usable protein (including fishmeal). Almost 60 percent of the
harvest was taken by only six countries: Peru, Japan, the
Soviet Union, mainland China, Norway, and the United States,
in that order.

Although world catch expanded by about 7 percent a year
for the decade prior to 1968, little or none of the fish protein
has been used to combat protein malnutrition in the poor
countries. Poor countries have lacked the purchasing power,
processing facilities, and distribution systems to create an effective demand for oceanic fish products. Even those poor
countries, like Peru, which have substantial fishing industries
do not utilize most of the catch domestically. Instead it is
converted into fishmeal and exported as livestock and poultry
feed to the rich countries to earn much-needed foreign exchange. But, some of the poor countries, like Mexico and Venezuela, are beginning to import fishmeal for their developing
poultry industries. It should be pointed out also that poultry
and pork, into which most fishmeal is converted, form the
mainstay of the poor man's animal protein in the rich countries.

Even with intensified fishing and greater yields, only a small
portion of man's calorie intake (around 1 percent) now comes
from the sea. But fish provide man with perhaps one-tenth of
his total protein supply and a far-higher proportion of the
world's animal protein.

The closer man has looked in recent years, the more apparent it has become that the ocean is not a limitless storehouse

of food forever there for the catching. Oceanographers and marine biologists have studied the ecological properties of the ocean, measured its marine life, considered the means of harvesting the sea's food resources, and concluded that severe constraints exist even to doubling the annual fish yield in the decades ahead.

The ocean, covering around 70 percent of the earth's surface, is not one equally fertile and productive ecosystem throughout. The open sea (an estimated 90 percent of the ocean) is considered a biological desert, contributing almost nothing to current world fishing and offering little potential for the future. Vast areas of clear, deep blue water form the Saharas of the ocean. Scarcity of water is not the problem, of course. Primary productivity is low in the open sea because nutrients are scarce in the upper layer, where light is sufficient for photosynthesis. And the phytoplankton found there, the tiny aquatic plants or photosynthetic producer organisms upon which all fish life in the ocean ultimately depends, are much smaller than varieties found in coastal waters. Food chains in the open sea are therefore longer, roughly five steps between phytoplankton and man. Fish of a size to be of interest to man as food are relatively few in number and widely dispersed. In contrast with the open sea, coastal waters are rich in nutrients, highly productive, and contain shorter food chains. Half of the oceanic fish supply of species useful to man is produced in coastal waters and a few fertile offshore regions, together comprising about 10 percent of the ocean area, but about 80 percent of the world fish harvest is landed in these waters. The most biologically productive regions of the ocean are the nutrient-rich upwelling areas such as those off the coast of Peru, California, and parts of Africa. Upwelling areas form only about 0.1 percent of the ocean but produce half of the oceanic fish supply.

Estimates of fish to be found annually in the sea, based on what is known of primary (photosynthetic) production of marine plants as well as conversion efficiencies along oceanic food chains, range from 200 million tons to 300 million tons of the species now utilized by man. Some estimates reach as high as 2 billion tons of marine animals large enough and useful enough to form the basis of commercial harvesting, but this assumes the future utilization of species farther down the oceanic food chain (for example, the Antarctic krill, the small crustaceans upon which whales feed and for which there now exist neither efficient harvesting technology nor markets). Annual production of fish in the sea, of course, far exceeds the potential biologically or economically feasible harvest. Man must be careful to leave a significant part of the annual fish population in order to assure a sustained maximum yield. Man must also take into account that fish have other predators, such as sea birds and seals, competing for the production. It is estimated, for example, that guano birds consume about 4 million tons of Peruvian anchovies each year.

John Rhyther of the Woods Hole Oceanographic Institute judges the potential economically sustainable fish harvest to be around 100 million tons annually. Others estimate that sustainable fish catch could reach between 150 and 200 million tons by the year 2000. It is doubtful that these latter amounts will be reached because of the costs of increased fishing effort, because of the as-yet incompletely understood effects of oceanic pollution, and because the pressure of man's current fishing is resulting in overexploitation and decline in several key commercial species. In 1969, after twenty consecutive annual increases, the world fish catch declined by 5 percent per capita. Since Japan and a few other nations have already claimed large portions of what turns out to be the limited natural food resources of the sea, reaching into the ocean for protein is not an uncontested alternative for protein-hungry, densely populated poor countries.

Some species that have declined are Antarctic blue whales, East Asian sardines, California sardines, Northwest Pacific salmon, Atlantic herring, Barents Sea cod, and Antarctic fin whales. Some stocks that are overfished in the sense that increased effort does not bring increased yield include tuna in the Atlantic, Pacific, and Indian Oceans; herring, cod, perch, flounder, and hake in the North Atlantic; anchovies in the southeastern Pacific; plaice and haddock in the North Sea and Barents Sea; and menhaden in the Atlantic, Pacific, and Indian oceans. This situation contrasts with 1949, when only a few species were considered overfished.

The overexploitation of whales has driven some species (blues and humpbacks) close to extinction. The Netherlands was forced to sell its whaling fleet to Japan in the mid-1960s, and Norway was forced out of the whaling industry in 1968, leaving only Russia and Japan. This is a sign of what may happen in other fisheries if the activities of man the fisher on the earth's last-remaining commons are not effectively regulated.

It is true that new fish stocks have been discovered in the Indian Ocean, the eastern Pacific, and even the intensely fished North Sea; but it is unlikely that these stocks will remain underexploited for very long. In fact, it is doubtful that any fish stocks of the species now utilized by man and accessible to current fishing techniques will remain underexploited in the decades ahead because of the exploding demand for protein and the pressure of population on the land.

With the intensity of modern fishing, the history of a fishery from modest beginning to overfishing is often compressed into a few years. The Peruvian anchoveta fishing industry is the example par excellence. Beginning in 1958, with the help of U.S. and Western European capital, Peru expanded its anchoveta fisheries in the rich Peruvian, or Humboldt, Current and catapulted upward in fish yields to become the largest fishing nation on earth by the early 1960s. By 1967, with a harvest of 10.5 million metric tons (metric ton = 2,204 pounds), which is nearly a sixth of the world tonnage, the anchoveta were already over-fished.

Maintaining an optimum level of oceanic productivity in the long run will depend in large part on not overexploiting fish stocks. Preventing overexploitation will, in turn, depend on how successful the human community is in creating an effective international system for managing the oceanic resources. As it stands now, competition among nations for fish resources and markets jeopardizes long-range planning. At least twenty regional or intergovernmental agencies for regulating fishing exist. But although fishing regulations are often agreed upon, enforcing them is difficult in the extreme. One example of a successful agreement that has averted overfishing is the joint control of Pacific halibut by Canada and the United States.

Even if it proves possible to double the world fish catch by improved but conventional fishing, this is far from a limitless increase. Going significantly beyond this limit would entail tapping oceanic food sources that are not now used because of economic or technical reasons. Fish stocks not currently utilized could be turned into fish protein concentrate (FPC), a flourlike fish additive heralded in recent years as a weapon in the war on protein hunger. The entire fish is ground up and the bony and fatty substances removed through chemical solvents; the result is an odorless, tasteless, high-protein powder. Although the potential for producing FPC is quite large, particularly when otherwise inedible species or parts of fish are used, there is no immediately foreseeable prospect that FPC will become commercially competitive with high-protein meals from plant sources such as soybeans or peanuts. Interestingly, the fish used for the first trial commercial batch of FPC, produced in 1969, was Atlantic hake, a species already overfished. The final product of this first run failed to meet protein standards demanded under the AID contract. Another objection to the trial batches was fluoride content high enough to produce tooth mottling, especially in children.

oceanic pollution

Besides being a source of food for man, the ocean serves as the great waste receptacle for the planet. Deliberately and accidentally, man is adding to the ocean many thousands of waste products—perhaps half a million different substances, many of which are highly toxic—via rivers, direct dumping, and windborne or rain-borne deposits. Among them are oil, chemical effluents, lethal chemical warfare gases, radioactive wastes, junk metal, trace elements, organic wastes from humans and animals, automobile exhaust products, pesticides, and detergents.

The long-term biological effects of polluting the ocean with industrial, military, municipal, and agricultural wastes are not yet fully known. Both the number and quantity of oceanic pollutants are growing faster than man's ability to collect information on them and their consequences, individually and synergistically, for the marine biosphere. It is certain, however, that oceanic pollution has reached alarming proportions in modern times, that it is planetary or global in scale, and that it poses an increasingly serious threat to the food resources of the sea.

It is well known that pollution of inland waters has killed some fish outright, jeopardized the existence of others, and rendered still others unfit to eat. In the rivers, lakes, and streams of the United States, for example, more than 15 million fish were killed by pollution in 1968, according to Interior Department estimates. Also, in 1969, 32,000 pounds of Coho salmon caught in Lake Michigan were banned from interstate commerce by the Food and Drug Administration (FDA) because of contamination by DDT.

Dangerous levels of mercury pollution, mainly from industrial wastes, were discovered in Lake Michigan as well as in the waters of at least thirty-three other states and Canada during 1970. As a result of mercury pollution, commercial and sport fishing were banned in many places, and the public was warned against eating fish from others. Early in 1971, quantities of tuna and swordfish were withdrawn from markets after high mercury levels were detected. The ubiquitous presence of mercury in the environment at levels seemingly higher than normal geochemical levels, particularly in a number of animals at the top of the food pyramid, has mystified and alarmed many. Mercury poisoning is insidious, causing a wide range of disorders from fatigue and headache to partial deafness, damage to the brain and nervous system, and death. Both illness and death have been blamed on mercury-tainted fish in Japan.

Fish are also known to pick up disease-causing organisms from human sewage, organisms that can then be passed back to humans when the fish are consumed. Organisms capable of causing typhoid fever, dysentery, and tuberculosis were found in Chesapeake Bay white perch. Thus the danger from contaminated fish, whether from freshwater or seawater, goes beyond the mere loss of food.

It is also known that some semiseparate parts of the ocean like the Baltic Sea, the Mediterranean, the Inland Sea of Japan, and the Gulf of Mexico are experiencing many forms of ecological imbalance due to mounting pollution. Some worry that the ocean, rather than becoming a greater food source in the future, will become another Lake Erie, eutrophic and productive of no edible food. The question is: What is the pollution threshold of the ocean beyond which the process of decay and death takes over? Because of the newness of oceanic pollution on a troublesome scale and because of the synergistic effects of various combinations of pollutants, no one knows.

Oil pollution is among the more serious threats to life in the sea. Approximately a million tons of oil have spilled from freighters, tankers, and oil rigs, according to estimates by Fred Singer, a former deputy assistant secretary in the Department of the Interior. But several million more tons of crude-oil products have been added to the ocean in the forms of gasoline, solvents, and waste motor oil. Oil spreads and has been found hundreds of miles from a spill area. It also persists for a long time before bacterial action dilutes it.

Oil floating on the surface interferes with the flow of light and air into the sea, making areas uninhabitable, at least temporarily. It also reduces evaporation, and since the bulk of usable freshwater comes from evaporation of ocean water, extensive and ineffectively controlled oil spills could presumably affect food production on the land. Populations of mollusks, seaweed, starfish, and various other shallow-water organisms have been destroyed or decimated in areas where there have been oil spills. The long-term effects of even low concentration of oil in the ocean may be even more hazardous to fish life than the more drastic short-term consequences are. Many fish species depend on smell to locate their prey and to find their way along migrational paths. The presence of oil interferes with these survival processes by masking smells and giving false cues, thus potentially threatening the survival of affected marine species and of other species linked to them in the food web.

Although thermal pollution—the runoff of hot water (at high temperatures) from power plants into the sea—has not yet reached critical levels and has rarely caused direct fish kills thus far, biologists are worried about its future effect on the ocean. There is a wealth of evidence on the sensitivity of fish to changes in water temperature as well as the susceptibility of marine ecosystems to disruption by such changes. In fact, temperature is a primary control of life on earth. Fish, cold-blooded creatures that they are, cannot regulate their body temperature and therefore cannot readily adjust to abrupt temperature changes, although they can adapt to temperature shifts within certain margins that are not too sudden. Water temperature affects the appetite, digestion, and growth of fish. It also affects their speed of movement and, hence, their ability to capture food or escape from predators. And it affects reproduction; above or below certain critical temperatures, fish will not reproduce. Marine ecosystems are even more sensitive to temperature variations than individual fish species are. Even seasonal warming of waters, particularly in the presence of sewage, can cause excessive blooms of some species of phytoplankton or algae, depleting the water of oxygen, at least temporarily, and producing other imbalances in the marine population. Any change in the marine environment that seriously affects the proliferation of any link in the food chain affects the relative abundance of other links.

Unless other methods for cooling condensers are developed, thermal pollution will worsen in the decade ahead, with the exhaustion of fossil fuels; the limited potential for hydroelectric, geothermal, and tidal power; and the increase of atomic energy production, now in its infancy.

Pesticides spread on the land find their way into estuaries and coastal waters, often far from their points of application, carried by rivers, rain, and winds. Winds have borne pesticides thousands of miles from the African continent to the Caribbean Sea and from various land areas to Antarctic ice. DDT is affecting shrimp, clams, oysters, as well as trout, salmon, and other fish. Even small amounts of DDT in water, a few parts per billion, can prevent reproduction in some species or greatly reduce numbers and size. The slightest amount of DDT in the water is lethal for shrimp. In 1968, it was found that a concentration of 8 parts per million in the ovaries of sea trout in an estuary off the Texas coast prevented spawning. Near Pensacola, the scallop population was wiped out several years ago after heavy DDT pollution. As little as 1 part in 10 billion of DDT in water can severely cut the growth rate of oysters. The problem is that DDT and related fat-soluble pesticides accumulate in aquatic organisms and are amplified along the food chain. Each predator or feeder along the way from plankton to bird, seal, and man concentrates the pesticide residues.

The effects of DDT on marine phytoplankton in nature are not clear at present. In the laboratory, DDT has been found to reduce photosynthesis in algae, diatoms, and other marine phytoplankton. Biologists feel that significant qualitative changes in the ocean's phytoplankton population are more probable than large reductions in the total quantity. If DDT proves capable of altering the relative abundance of phytoplankton species, causing some to bloom and others to decline, repercussions would be felt throughout the marine food web, fostering the proliferation of some fish species and the reduction of others.

farming the sea

In the sea, man remains a hunter, chasing fish shoals, gathering mollusks, trapping lobsters. Man dreams of farming the ocean expanses with methods similar to those used on land. He wants to raise the productivity of the sea through fertilizing, transplanting species, causing fish to reproduce in captivity, regulating temperature, removing pests, and controlling disease. He dreams of eventually cultivating the sea bed with giant tractors and raising fish in compounds surrounded by electric fences. Significant technological advances on a small scale have already appeared. Certain marine species such as clams and oysters have been farmed for centuries. The famous Pacific Ocean, or California, oyster is actually a transplant from the Atlantic waters off the eastern coast of the United States. But in recent years, the Japanese have, remarkably, conditioned trout from the fingerling stage to gather on sonic impulses to feed at a chosen spot, even if the fish are spread in open waters. The Soviets have done the same for cod in the Barents Sea. Japanese scientists have proposed herding and raising tuna in closed-off Pacific Ocean atolls and lagoons. Similarly, Gifford B. Pinchot, a Johns Hopkins University biologist, has suggested the creation of whale farms using circular coral atolls in the Pacific as pens or corrals. If this were accomplished, whales would be preserved and their numbers multiplied. The benefit to man's diet would be enormous, since the whale is the largest animal ever to have lived on earth—larger than the dinosaur or elephant. Meat from a blue whale may be equivalent to that from fifteen to twenty steers.

The big problem with herding whales or fish is food supply. Experimental advances have been made with the technology of providing food for fish being raised in ocean pens. Pinchot suggests using windmills to pump nutrient-rich deep water into atolls to promote growth of plankton, the food of whales. On Saint Croix, Columbia University scientists are carrying out an experiment with oysters that resembles Pinchot's plan for whales. Oysters (and perhaps eventually snails, shrimp, and anchovies) are being raised on phytoplankton that is grown in pools fed by nutrient-rich seawater pumped from depths of half a mile. Scientists are also exploring the possibility of artificially creating large upwelling areas similar to the fertile Humboldt Current upwelling region off Peru. And further experiments and plans to systematically control whole regions of the ocean, such as the Caribbean, are being evaluated in the drawing-board stage.

Domestication, of course, ultimately includes the ability of marine species to function sexually in captivity, as many freshwater fish do. Israelis, by injecting pituitary hormones, have caused mullets to spawn under artificial conditions. The same or similar techniques may eventually be applied to other as yet undomesticated marine species.

If left uncontrolled, oceanic pollution will be a growing obstacle to obtaining food from the sea by farming as well as by nomadic fishing. Unfortunately, contamination of the ocean by industrial effluents, agricultural chemicals, and oil is greatest in estuaries, bays, and coastal waters, precisely those areas best suited for marine farming.

Some forms of pollution have potential usefulness for the culture of marine animals and plants. Many wastes are nutrients. Put in the right places in the right quantities and composition, mineral-rich sewage could be made to work as fertilizer in ocean farming without damaging the marine environment. Sewage has been used effectively in carp ponds of Asia and southern Germany. Thermal pollution is also promising as a potential aid in farming the ocean. Warmer waters along the Scottish coast have attracted new species of fish formerly found in warmer latitudes. The harnessing of warmwater outfall of coastal power plants might eventually make temperature control of seawater possible in some areas, thus producing optimum growth in the size and quantity of certain species, such as trout. Temperature control is now being used effectively in about 100 saltwater fish farms along the northwestern coast of Norway.

Making the ocean into the farm of the future has several severe constraints besides growing pollution and insufficient technology. Inadequate knowledge is another problem. Man's knowledge of the oceans is still in its infancy, although marine science is expanding rapidly. Oceanographic studies of recent decades have greatly enlarged understanding of currents, underwater topography, temperature, light, and salt conditions. Man has discovered more about the feeding, reproductive, and migrational patterns of fish. He has gained insight into the complicated ecological interrelationships that exist in the underwater world. Just this growth in knowledge makes many informed men cautious and tentative in their evaluation of the prospects for farming the ocean. Georg Borgstrom, a leading food scientist and fisheries expert, feels that man is a long way from systematic cultivation of the ocean expanses:

Despite all these impressive advances we still know far too little to make the radical shift to systematic cultivation of fish. The truth is rather the opposite; increased knowledge has dampened the enthusiasm and given us a more realistic picture of the intricate and complex conditions under which the oceans produce and maintain life. *

Economic and political factors also dim prospects for farming the ocean on a large scale in the near future. Since the ocean remains a commons, and since fish are highly mobile and capricious, no one nation is willing to pour capital into sowing a harvest it cannot be certain of reaping. Even before 1905, successful fish-transplanting experiments were carried out in the coastal waters near Holland. Thousands of young plaice were trawled up from the crowded coastal banks of Holland and transported in tanks to the Dogger bank, where they were released after being marked and measured. On recapture they were found to have grown three or four times as much as those studied in the original coastal waters. Estimated costs of transplanting millions of young fish would not have preempted substantial profit. Without international cooperation, however, the endeavor was not economically practical for the investing nation in 1905, nor would it be today.

summary

Sea husbandry is doubtless coming—provided man controls oceanic pollution—although certainly not fast enough nor on a scale large enough to make a significant contribution to world protein shortages in the near future. The transition from fisherman to farmer of the ocean is not imminent. Man's hope for the more immediate future lies not with the ocean but with increasing the productivity of the land.

*Georg Borgstrom, *The Hungry Planet* (New York: Macmillan, 1965), p. 376.

the ocean as a
source of food

SUGGESTED READINGS

Bardach, John E., "Aquaculture," *Science*, September 3, 1968.

Borgstrom, Georg, *The Hungry Planet*, New York: Macmillan, 1965.

Clark, John R. "Thermal Pollution and Aquatic Life," *Scientific American*, March, 1969.

Ehrlich, Paul, and Anne H. Ehrlich, *Population, Resources, Environment: Issues in Human Ecology*, San Francisco: W. H. Freeman, 1970.

Holt, S. J., "The Food Resources of the Ocean," *Scientific American*, September, 1969.

Ovington, J. D., *The Better Use of the World's Fauna for Food*, London: Institute of Biology, 1964.

President's Science Advisory Committee, *The World Food Problem*, Report of the Panel on the World Food Supply, vol. 2, Washington, D.C.: U.S. Government Printing Office, 1967.

Rhyther, John H., "Photosynthesis and Food Production in the Sea," *Science*, October 3, 1969.

Ricker, William E., "Food from the Sea," in *Resources and Man*, Committee on Man, National Academy of Sciences-National Research Council, San Francisco: W. H. Freeman, 1969.

Taylor, Gordon Rattray, "The Threat to Life in the Sea," *Saturday Review*, August 1, 1970.

Wurster, C. F., "DDT Reduces Photosynthesis by Marine Phytoplankton," *Science*, February 7, 1968.

8
land-use
patterns

For two million years or more, man has been dependent upon the land for the bulk of his food. Man will continue to be dependent largely upon land for food in the foreseeable future. Man also depends on the sea. But, as pointed out earlier, fish and other marine life provide only a minor portion of his food energy, although a much greater portion of his protein supply. *Hydroponics*, or plant culture without soil, has been technically possible for a long time, but is too costly to be economically practical on a large scale. And most of the nutrients used to feed plants raised hydroponically must be extracted from the soil.

Current advances in growing single-cell organisms on petroleum may have far-reaching implications for conventional agriculture and man's traditional dependence on the land. Several large international petroleum companies are funding extensive research and development programs designed to produce both animal feed and human food. Should this effort prove successful, man may some day refer to population/petroleum ratios as well as to population/land ratios. Within Latin America, for example, Venezuela, with its vast oil reserves, could become

Argentina's principal competitor as an exporter of feedstuffs and foodstuffs. But it is too soon to assess the potentialities of this exotic food-producing technology.

agricultural land
resources

The earth's total land surface is estimated to be 32.9 billion acres. Man has removed the natural cover and extended cultivation to some 3.5 billion acres, planting the food, fiber, and tree crops he has domesticated. This amounts to only about 10 percent of the earth's total land area, and it, watered and fertilized by man as well as by nature, supports the entire human population of 3.5 billion and a large portion of man's livestock population. Expressed in these terms, the area cleared by man seems small. But man's cropland amounts to a considerably larger fraction of the earth's land surface actually capable of supporting vegetation, that is, the area excluding polar regions, deserts, and higher elevations. In terms of the land area potentially capable of supporting crops useful to man, it is still larger.

Although the earth's cultivated or arable area extends to 3.5 billion acres, considerably less than this amount (usually under 2.4 billion acres, or around 7 percent of the world's land area) is actually planted to crops in any given year. The difference between arable land and the land area actually planted in any one year is, by definition, fallow land and land in temporary pastures. Permanent meadows and pastures that are suitable for grazing amount to 6.4 billion acres, or 19 percent of the earth's land surface. Agricultural land, including both arable land and permanent pastures, currently adds up to 30 percent of the earth's land surface.

The 70 percent of the earth's land not classified as agricultural land may not be naturally well suited to agriculture for many reasons, but moisture and temperature are the major constraining factors. Much of the world is too dry to support flourishing plant life. The Sahara desert covers a large part of the African continent. The Thar Desert, covering the northwestern corner of the Indo-Pakistan subcontinent, is larger than the combined cultivated areas of East and West Pakistan. Huge areas of China and Mongolia are covered by the vast Gobi desert. The interior of Australia is largely desert and wasteland. Deserts are somewhat less common in Europe and the Western Hemisphere, although large dry areas do exist in southern Europe, coastal Peru, northeastern Brazil, Central America, and in the North American Southwest.

When rainfall is not a limiting factor, land may be located at elevations too high or in regions too cold to support commercial crops: for example, the North American Rocky Mountains, the South American Andes, the European Alps, the vast Asian Himalayan plateau, and the extensive northern latitudes of Canada and the Soviet Union.

If the earth's arable lands were placed end to end around the equator, they would form a belt only 200 miles wide. Oceans, it will be recalled, cover 70 percent of the earth's surface; and polar caps, mountains, tundra, and deserts cover a large portion of the land area. The earth's arable land is distributed very unevenly among the world's major regions. Asia, with 31 percent, has the largest share, followed by Eastern Europe (including the Soviet Union), with almost 20 percent; Africa, with nearly 17 percent; North America, with around 16 percent; and Latin America and Western Europe, with approximately 7 percent each. Oceania contains only 2 percent. With the exception of the Argentine Pampas, the great bulk of the arable land lies north of the equator. The Gangetic plain of India, continental Western Europe, the region of the United States east of the Rocky Mountains, and the Pampas of Argentina are the largest concentrations of fertile agricultural land on the planet.

Across the surface of the earth, population and arable land do not encounter each other in equal proportions. Although Asia has almost one-third of the world's arable land, this densely populated region contains more than half the world's population, thanks, in large part, to the carrying capacity of rice fields. Communist Asia alone accounts for nearly one-quarter of the human population, more people than live in the Western Hemisphere, Africa, and western Asia combined.

Western Europe's share of the world's population is also larger than its share of arable land. But all other regions (Africa, North America, Eastern Europe, and Oceania) have smaller shares of population than of arable land, except Latin America, which has identical shares, around 7 percent, of the world's population and arable area.

Some of the world's geographic regions have low proportions of arable land. Even with the Argentine Pampas, only 5 percent of Latin America's area is currently listed as arable, whereas as much as 28 percent of Europe's land is arable. Australia and Canada currently cultivate only 3–4 percent of their lands, although they are both leading surplus-food producers. Within geographic regions, some countries have much greater proportions of land suitable for cultivating than others do. In Western Europe, for example, France, Germany, the Netherlands, and Belgium have generous amounts of arable land, whereas only 2–3 percent of Norway's land can be cultivated. In Asia, vastly unequal shares of the land of India and China are considered arable: 49 percent in India and only 11 percent in China. The same unevenness of spread of arable land is found in South America, where only 2 percent of Brazil is now cultivated, compared with 17 percent of Cuba.

Permanent meadow and pasture lands, grazing lands supporting wild and domestic animals, are almost double the arable land area of the world. Grazing lands exceed croplands by varying amounts in all the world's major geographic areas except Western Europe. Africa, with its vast stretches of savanna, contains the largest portion of the earth's grazing area. But all geographic regions have substantial expanses of grazing land. Compared with the earth's arable land, grazing land tends to be drier, located at higher elevations, rockier, and steeper.

By nature, the quality or productive capacity of land is determined by a large number of interacting environmental factors: principally moisture, temperature, latitude, drainage, soil structure, cloud cover, alkalinity, salinity, and mineral composition of the soil. Blanket statements cannot be made about the quality of much of the earth's land because fertility or productive capacity is not constant, but variable. It varies with crops or strains of crop plants and with man's ability to alter or systematically manage both crops and environmental factors.

A region of heavy rainfall, for example, would never produce tea, but might be ideal for rice. Similarly, much of the dry American Great Plains would not naturally support corn, but is highly productive when small grains (wheat, oats, barley, rye, sorghum) are planted. In the future, man's ability to match crops to land rationally and his ability to breed more efficient and productive plant varieties suited to particular soils and climates will greatly determine the land's productive capacity. Once arctic regions could not support grains. But now Scandinavia is growing improved strains of wheat near the Arctic Circle. American farmers can raise corn 500 miles farther north than they could formerly because of new corn strains. Current efforts to map the earth's soils should aid in rationalizing agriculture along these lines.

Cropping patterns change over time, of course. Dark rye bread has been the staple food of European peasantry for centuries. Tastes have changed, however, and today dark bread is being rejected by European peasants and wheat bread is preferred instead. As a consequence, the crop area planted to rye is declining while that planted to wheat is increasing.

expanding the cultivated area

There are possibilities for expanding the world's cultivated area, but only at substantial costs. The fact that more and more of the increases in world food output come from increasing yields on land already under the plow rather than expanding the cultivated area is an indication of the great costs.

Little, if any, potential for new farmlands exists in Europe and Asia, apart from regions of Burma, Indonesia, the Philippines, and Thailand. The world's most populous countries— mainland China and India in Asia and the Soviet Union in Europe—are finding it difficult to add to the cultivated area. Efforts to bring land under cultivation there mainly take the

land-use patterns

form of large-scale cooperative or government projects involving irrigation, drainage, or clearing land with heavy machinery. The Soviet Union has had to abandon some of the land plowed up in the late 1950s during the expansion into virgin lands. Most countries of North Africa and the Middle East, dependent as they are on irrigation or dryland farming, cannot significantly expand the area under cultivation without developing new sources of irrigation water.

In several countries of the world, the area of cultivated land is actually declining. For example, in Japan, this area reached a peak in 1920 and has declined substantially ever since. Some countries in Western Europe, notably Sweden, Norway, Ireland, and Switzerland, have been losing agricultural land to the construction of highways, airfields, factories, and homes for the past several decades. Land now being farmed in many parts of the developing world is marginal and should be withdrawn from cultivation because soils are being depleted and destroyed.

The United States is the only country in the world that in recent years has had a ready reserve of idled cropland, around 50 million acres, compared with a harvested area of 300 million acres. This idled acreage has served as the safety valve of the world in recent decades when the need for imported food and feed was growing in Western Europe, Eastern Europe, Japan, India, and many other poor countries. But farmland is being lost in the United States, too, because of expanding urban areas, the construction of highways, the building of airstrips, the creation of reservoirs and public recreation areas, and other developments.

The inherent productive capacity of land can be greatly altered by careful management. Japan, for example, extracts some of the world's highest yields from land that is either inherently infertile or, at best, not notably fertile. This exemplary feat has involved painstaking effort in the form of drainage, irrigation projects, and the use of large quantities of both traditional organic fertilizer and, more recently, chemical fertilizers. Japanese farmers have applied good management and large quantities of capital to attain yield levels two to four times as high as farmers elsewhere in the world with land of comparable inherent fertility.

cropping patterns

How is the earth's crop acreage currently used? Most of the world's cropland is devoted to raising a relatively small number of crops (Figure 6). More than two-thirds of the cultivated cropland is planted to cereals: wheat, rice, corn, millet, sorghum, barley, oats, and rye. Wheat alone covers more than a fifth of man's cultivated land area. Although the amount of land planted to rice is only about half the wheat acreage, the world's total production of both grains is approximately the same, since rice yield per acre is much higher, perhaps 70 percent, than wheat yield. The difference in yield reflects the fact that most of the world's wheat is grown in low-rainfall areas, whereas most rice is grown in heavy-rainfall areas. Wheat and rice are cultivated mainly as food for man, but much of the remaining grain output is used as fodder for livestock. Of the total area planted to grains, perhaps one-third is used to produce livestock feed.

Next to grains, oilseeds are the most important group of commodities, and they utilize 7 percent of the world's har-

figure 6. *World harvested area of principal crops. (From U.S. Department of Agriculture.)*

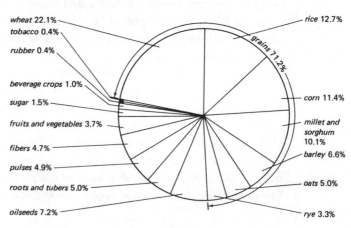

vested area. Roots, tubers, pulses, and fibers follow, with shares of about 5 percent each. Fruits and vegetables use a surprisingly small portion of the harvested area: 3.7 percent. And coffee, tea, and cocoa occupy only 1 percent of the area.

Edible crops now occupy more than 94 percent of the earth's farmland. Only around 5 percent of the cropland is devoted to growing inedible crops. Fibers, mainly cotton, account for most of this. Tobacco and rubber take very small portions of the crop-producing land, about 0.4 percent each. Even if it were possible to replace rubber and fibers entirely with synthetics, the area thereby released for food production would not be large. Tobacco, rubber, and beverage crops, although occupying less than 2 percent of the world's cropland, account for about one-fifth of the value of total agricultural exports.

Sub-Saharan Africa and the Amazon basin of Brazil are the only major regions where there are sizable portions of well-watered, potentially arable land. Any substantial expansion in these two areas awaits further improvements in man's ability to manage tropical soils once the lush, protective natural vegetation is removed. Mineral nutrients are easily leached from most tropical soils by heavy rainfall once the natural cover is gone. The soil that remains is red or yellow in color and rich in iron oxide and alumina. Such soil is not only relatively infertile but is also converted to a bricklike rock, known as laterite, when exposed to sun and air. The process of laterization is thought to have undermined the great Khmer civilization in Cambodia centuries ago. Laterite was used to build the magnificent temples of Angkor Wat. In less than five years, laterization turned farm fields into rock at Iata, Brazil, the Brazilian government's experimental agricultural colony.

summary

Apart from the above possibilities, no further opportunities to expand farm areas are likely to arise until the cost of desalinization is reduced to the point where it is profitable to use seawater to irrigate coastal deserts, or until it is technically possible and economically feasible to alter rainfall patterns to shift some of the rainfall normally occurring on the oceans to arid land masses capable of being farmed. This will probably not occur for another decade or two at best.

The fact is that man is already occupying and farming most of the best and readily cultivable land of the earth. His hope for the years immediately ahead is to raise the productivity of that land.

SUGGESTED READINGS

Brown, Lester R., *Man, Land, Food*, Washington, D. C.: U. S. Government Printing Office, 1963.

Hendricks, Sterling B., "Food from the Land," in *Resources and Man*, Committee on Resources and Man, National Academy of Sciences–National Research Council, San Francisco, W. H. Freeman, 1969.

President's Science Advisory Committee, *The World Food Problem*, Report of the Panel on the World Food Supply, vol. 2, Washington, D. C.: U. S. Government Printing Office, 1967.

9
the area-to-yield transition

There are two major ways to expand the food supply: (1) bring more land under the plow or (2) raise yields on land already under cultivation. During all but the last 20 of the 10,000–12,000 years that man has been practicing agriculture, increases in the world food supply have come largely from expanding the cultivated area. Globally, and throughout history, increases in output per acre were scarcely perceptible within any given generation. Only during the twentieth century have more and more countries succeeded in achieving rapid, continuing increases in output per acre, culminating in a global turning point in the man-land–food relationship. Since 1950, increases in the world food supply have come more from the rising productivity of land than from expanding the land area under cultivation (Figure 7).

chemical fertilizers

Scientific advances in soil chemistry and in plant genetics over the past two centuries have given man powerful tools for intervening in the earth's ecosystem more extensively than ever before in his quest for food. Early in the nineteenth century, the German chemist Justus von

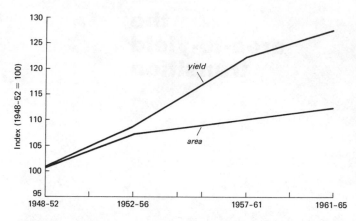

figure 7. *World grain: indexes of area and yield. Since about 1950 around 70 percent of worldwide increases in grain production have resulted from rising grain yields. Only about 30 percent of the increases have resulted from expanding the area planted to grain. (From U.S. Department of Agriculture.)*

Liebig, known as the father of modern soil chemistry, laid the foundations for a major technological advance in agriculture: the development and use of chemical fertilizers. Von Liebig identified the importance of the major nutrients in plant growth, particularly nitrogen, phosphorus, and potassium. He demonstrated that the natural fertility of soil could be enhanced or restored by adding these nutrients in required or proper proportions and recommended the use of mineral (i.e., chemical or inorganic) fertilizers in farming.

At the time of von Liebig's findings, the land resources in much of the world still provided ample opportunity for expanding the area under cultivation. When population increased and more food was required, more land was brought under the plow to produce it. Application of chemical fertilizers did not become widespread until this century, when the pressure of population and the disappearance of frontiers compelled man to substitute fertilizer for expansion of cropland to meet mounting food needs. As of 1970, the world's farmers were using roughly 70 million metric tons of plant nutrients on 3 billion acres of cropland, about 47 pounds per acre. Some of the adverse consequences of this usage for the earth's ecosystem are discussed in Chapters 12 and 13.

Chemical-fertilizer usage varies widely among countries and geographic regions, however (Table 3). In some poor countries, chemical fertilizers are scarcely used at all. But in densely populated industrial countries located in temperate regions with high rainfall, usage is intensive. The application of chem-

table 3

consumption of commercial fertilizers (world use of the commercial fertilizers N, P_2O_5, and K_2O, in terms of nutrient content)[a]

	average 1952/53– 1956/57	1966/67	consumption per hectare arable land, kilograms, 1966/67
Western Europe	7.5	13.9	134
Eastern Europe and USSR	3.5	11.2	39
North America	5.9	13.5	61
Oceania	0.7	1.6	41
Japan	1.1	2.1	350
Total for developed countries (including Israel and S. Africa)	18.8	42.7	64
Latin America	0.5	1.8	17
Far East (excluding Japan and Mainland China)	0.6	2.7	10
Near East	0.2	0.7	16
Africa	0.1	0.4	2
Total for developing countries	1.4	5.6	9
World Total	20.2	48.3	36

[a]Data are given in million tons.

Source: Food and Agriculture Organization of the United Nations, 1968. *The State of Food and Agriculture 1968,* Rome: FAO, 1968.

ical fertilizers in combination with other inputs and practices can double, triple, or quadruple the soil's productivity in high-rainfall or intensively irrigated areas. In countries practicing intensive agriculture, such as Japan or the Netherlands, chemical fertilizers are applied at more than 300 pounds per acre yearly and account for a large share of the food supply. Stated otherwise, if the use of chemical fertilizers was discontinued in these countries, soil fertility would decline rapidly, and food production would drop by perhaps half or more. If the use of chemical fertilizers was discontinued on a global basis, man's total food supply would probably be reduced by at least one-fourth.

Although there is much nitrogen in the atmosphere, it is present in a gaseous state that is not assimilable by higher plants or animals, both of which require nitrogen. In nature, the nitrogen of the air is changed into an available form in the soil by certain bacteria (microorganisms), the best known of which are the nitrogen-fixing bacteria associated with nodules on roots of leguminous plants. Historically, agriculturalists often designed crop rotations to include a leguminous plant (such as clover, alfalfa, soybeans, or peanuts) to periodically restore or boost the soil's natural fertility. During the current century, man has learned to speed up the nitrogen-fixing phase of the nitrogen cycle. Through various chemical processes, man can inexpensively synthesize atmospheric nitrogen into inorganic compounds. The result is low-cost nitrogen that can be applied to soil in the form of nitrogen fertilizer (such as ammonium sulfate or ammonium nitrate), making the application of nitrogen fertilizer more economic and rapid than the use of leguminous crops in rotation. Man is now synthesizing and adding to the earth's soil more than 40 million tons of nitrogen fertilizer annually.

If global projections of population and income growth materialize, fertilizer production over the next three decades must nearly triple in order to satisfy food demands. The supply of nitrogen in the atmosphere is seemingly without limit. In the case of potassium or potash (K_2O), reserves in the rich, vast potash fields in Canada alone are expected to be sufficient to meet man's needs for centuries to come.

The nutrient that is least plentiful and most likely to become a constraining factor in food production is phosphorus. Some 3.5 million tons of phosphorus wash into the ocean each year from the earth's land masses. Man has accelerated this one-way flow through mining the phosphorus reserves found on land. Unlike nitrogen, neither phosphorus nor potassium is replenished by cycling back into the atmosphere or onto land. Although continental reserves of potassium are abundant, those of phosphorus are not. Phosphorus becomes sediment on the ocean floor and will eventually be thrust above the ocean surface through geological uplift. But this is a very long-term natural phenomenon. In the short run, it will not alleviate any shortages. If a great demand for the mining of nutrients from the ocean bed arises, the economic pressures to mine phosphorus might be among the earlier ones to develop. Marine deposits exist that are not too inaccessible, but their extent is not known.

plant genetics

The second major breakthrough of the nineteenth century that has contributed enormously to the earth's food-producing capacity is the breakthrough in plant genetics made possible by Gregor Johann Mendel's experiments with the garden pea. In 1857, Mendel began to crossbreed garden pea plants and tabulate the results. After eight years, he formulated a series of laws governing genetic inheritance and published an account of his experiments and his results in a paper that was ignored for decades. When the paper was discovered by three young biologists after his death, it fostered a revolution in genetics, giving man a great boost in his efforts to breed crops and livestock for greater productivity.

Through selecting and favoring desired strains, man remarkably altered, over millennia, the genetic compositions of the plant and animal species that he domesticated. The extraordinary development of corn by New World Indians is a case in point. Not only did they eventually enlarge strawberry-size corn ears containing only eight rows of forty to fifty kernels each to ears measuring 6–8 inches with seventeen rows and many more kernels, but, from an original Central American domesticate, they differentiated and developed varieties that could survive and flourish in an amazing variety of North and South American soils, climates, and habitats.

With knowledge of genetics, man has become a biological engineer breeding plants to specifications by drawing upon germ plasm from varying sources and greatly accelerating evolutionary development in the process. Building on the work of Mendel and others, plant breeders in the current century have learned to select, classify, and combine literally dozens of plant characteristics in order to alter them. They can make plants shorter or taller, more responsive to fertilizer, more resistant to drought, more tolerant of cold, more resistant to disease; they can change the quantity and quality of protein and the cooking characteristics of various crops. For example, they have extended the northern limit of commercial corn production some 500 miles within the United States, developed wheats that would yield well near the equator, and increased the oil content of soybeans; and they have begun to develop entirely new, man-made cereals.

Since 1888, plant breeders have known about triticale, a cross between wheat and rye, with exceptionally high protein yield, first bred in Germany. Until 1968, the development of triticale had been held up by two problems: partial sterility and a high incidence of shriveled grain. Within the last two years, however, highly fertile lines and lines with superior grain types have been discovered. If these two characteristics can be combined, triticale may soon be competitive with established cereals. An estimated 200,000 acres were planted to triticale during 1970–1971 in the United States. Exciting possibilities of developing other man-made cereals also exist.

yield takeoff

In order to coax significantly higher yields from an acre of land in the twentieth century, the technologies in agricultural chemistry and plant breeding developed earlier were applied on a commercial basis. In combination with other inputs and practices, they have played the central roles in man's ability to markedly raise crop yields.

The first yield-per-acre takeoff, a transition from a condition of near-static yields to one of rapid and continuing increases in yields, probably occurred in Japan around the turn of the century. But some of the smaller, more densely populated northwestern European countries, such as Denmark and the Netherlands, may also have engendered yield takeoffs around the same time.

Japan's yield takeoff was not as dramatic as those experienced by several countries around 1940 and, more recently, in the late 1960s. In the last decade of the nineteenth century, Japan had already brought into production most of its cultivable land. As pointed out in Chapter 7, this densely populated archipelagic country was forced to turn to the oceans for protein and use its limited land resources for producing starchy staples, principally rice, to meet food-energy needs. At that time, Japan was essentially a fixed-land agricultural economy that was just beginning to industrialize. The population was still growing, and large-scale emigration was not possible because, even at that early date, opportunities for emigration were more limited for Asians than for Europeans.

Given the fixed-land situation and continuing population growth, Japan faced the alternatives of intensifying cultivation of existing rice fields in an effort to increase yields, of growing more dependent on food imports, or of accepting a decline in per capita food consumption that would have led to increasing malnutrition. Either of the latter alternatives would have hindered Japan's economic development. Japan chose the first alternative, and this early realization that higher yields were essential for the country's overall development was indispensable to the subsequent upward trend in rice yields. Through intensive farming, rice yields began to rise in the early years of this century, and have risen steadily year by year for seven decades, except during war (Figure 8).

How was Japan able to execute the area-to-yield transition at

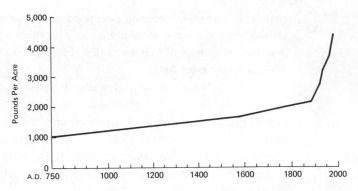

figure 8. *Rice yields in Japan: A.D. 750–1960. Historical estimates from the Japanese Ministry of Agriculture. (From U.S. Department of Agriculture.)*

such an early stage of development? In Japan, the policy of generating a yield takeoff was supported by government at national, provincial, and local levels from the time of the Meiji restoration of 1868. The unification of some 200 rather loosely federated feudal baronies scattered throughout many islands facilitated the agricultural modernization effort. The national government, recognizing that some individual farmers and communities were advanced agriculturally and that others were quite backward, actively sought, and supported the spread of, the more advanced indigenous farming practices. Japanese officials were also sent abroad to England, Germany, and the United States to search for improved farming techniques that could be applied to Japanese agriculture. The transfer of technology was not always smooth because technologies designed for large-scale western farms had to be adapted to Japan's small, garden-size farms. Japan's greatest gain came from learning about chemical fertilizers and methods of application.

Although the abundant and skillful use of chemical fertilizer was the major factor in the Japanese rice-yield takeoff, the fertilizers had to be used in conjunction with other inputs and practices in order to be effective. The Japanese also improved irrigation, drainage, and water storage; extended irrigation to more cropland; and worked toward developing new rice varieties that would be more responsive to fertilizer. They also devised the Japanese paddy method for growing rice, a method of setting rice plants in rows in order to permit cultivating between rows. Planting in rows results in more uniform stands, better ventilation, and optimum plant density And plants grown in this manner both require and have the ability to utilize heavy applications of fertilizer and water. To make investment in fertilizer and other technologies possible, the Japanese developed price supports.

Generating a yield takeoff is difficult for any country and requires an abrupt departure from traditional ways of farming. It was not until 1940 that another group of countries, including the United Kingdom, the United States, and Australia, generated yield-per-acre takeoffs. These were economically advanced countries either with much cultivable land in relation to population or with national policies that discriminated against agriculture while attempting to develop industry.

The United Kingdom was among the latter, but the U-boat threat during World War II reversed this policy, accomplishing what centuries of gradual advances in farm technology had not. It stimulated a leap upward in agricultural productivity unique in the history of this populous industrial nation. Heavily dependent on grain imports, the United Kingdom was pushed to the wall when its food supply lines were severed. Britishers moved into action quickly to expand food output on their own land. Acreage planted to grains (wheat, oats, and barley) nearly doubled in the early 1940s. But surprisingly, per-acre grain yields did not decline, as they often do when cultivation is extended to more marginal land; they increased rapidly. This dramatic expansion of grain lands, plus the more modest but extremely significant rise in per-acre yields, doubled output.

The gains in output per acre turned out to be not a temporary response or a new plateau, but a sharp change from centuries of almost-static yields or barely noticeable increases. Yields per acre continued to shoot upward rapidly. Historically ranging between 700 and 800 kg per acre, they climbed beyond 900 kg in 1942. By 1949, when grain yields exceeded

1,000 kg, it was clear that an extraordinary takeoff in output per acre had occurred in the early 1940s. In 1963, yields per acre reached nearly 1,400 kg.

But as remarkable as this takeoff was, it is surprising that it did not take place in the United Kingdom until the 1940s. England had practiced agriculture since the first bands of farmers arrived on its southern shores, perhaps earlier than 3000 B.C. And this island had cradled the technological revolution that for the last 200 years has been spreading over the globe, affecting industry and agriculture on all continents. England, in contrast with Japan, had placed priorities on developing industry, exporting manufactured goods in exchange for foodstuffs and industrial raw materials. Population growth had characterized Britain, but large numbers had migrated to other parts of the world. Improvements in agriculture centered on mechanization and were designed primarily to save labor, not to raise the productivity of land.

It took the crisis of World War II to spur the United Kingdom to concentrate on, and bend efforts toward, intensifying cultivation sufficiently to generate a yield takeoff. Chemical fertilizers and improved grain varieties were the principal inputs. But various land-improvement practices such as field drainage systems and rock removal, strategic use of machinery, and government price supports also contributed. Economic conditions, namely highly favorable prices for farm products, proved to be the key factor in bringing the accumulated technologies into play.

During the latter part of the nineteenth century, when Japan was generating a takeoff in rice yields per acre, the United States, a highly diversified grain producer, was still pushing its frontier westward. The period was one of dramatic expansion of grain-producing area, first reaching beyond the heavily settled eastern states into the midwestern belt, and then gradually filling up the vast expanses of the Great Plains. It was not until just before World War I that settlement of the frontier ended.

Ecologically, the United States is exceptionally well favored to produce food crops. Its midwestern corn belt is one of the largest areas of fertile, moist farmland in the world. Only the

Pampas of Argentina, the Gangetic plain of India, and northwestern Europe even remotely approach it in size and inherent
fertility.

Over the more than seven decades from just after the Civil
War to the years immediately preceding World War II, grain
yields per acre remained essentially unchanged. This was true
despite the fact that the United States tried for two and a half
decades after the closing of the frontier to make the transition
from the area-expanding to the yield-raising method of increasing food output. Per-acre crop yields finally began to rise
around 1940, and have continued to trend upward.

A host of interwoven factors, found in varying combinations
with individual grains, are responsible for the takeoff in yields
in the United States: hybrid varieties of corn and, later, sorghum, growing use of chemical fertilizers and pesticides, efficient modern farm equipment, government price incentives,
and acreage controls that removed much marginal land from
production. In the broadest sense, the American yield takeoff
was the result of the massive application of accumulated scientific knowledge and technology to agriculture. Once the yield
takeoff was under way first in corn (Figures 9 and 10) and
then in other grains, American agriculture was modernized at
an unprecedented rate. Although no one factor wholly accounts for the successful area-to-yield transition, the hybrid
varieties of corn and sorghum played unique roles in the American experience.

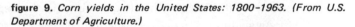

figure 9. *Corn yields in the United States: 1800–1963. (From U.S.
Department of Agriculture.)*

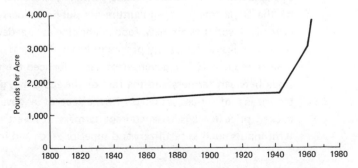

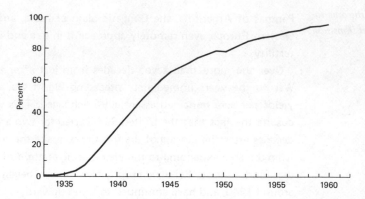

figure 10. *Share of U.S. corn acreage planted with hybrid seed. (From U.S. Department of Agriculture.)*

the role of government

Careful delineation of the role of government also contributed importantly to the success of American agriculture. Government has never been directly engaged in agricultural production, nor in producing and distributing any of the multitude of inputs that modern agriculture requires. Actions such as the Homestead Act of 1862 were designed specifically to encourage private settlement and production. The U.S. government's role has included agricultural research, education, and the extension of new techniques from the laboratory and experimental plot to the farm. The first publicly supported agricultural research took place before the Civil War under the sponsorship of the Patent Office (later to become the Department of Agriculture). Discoveries made through research sponsored by the Department of Agriculture are public property. When new plant varieties or new food technologies are developed, they are released for use by private industry.

Since the late 1930s, government has influenced the terms of trade between farmers and the rest of the economy, generally by means of price supports. The effect of a government-backed price level is to encourage farmers to invest in short-term inputs such as fertilizers and superior seeds and in longer-term inputs such as irrigation, drainage, land improvement, and machinery. Governments in nearly all countries with modern, intensive agriculture operate price-support programs for principal crops.

How high yields of the major food crops upon which man depends for sustenance can or will go by the year 2000 is very difficult to say. This may depend more on economic factors such as strength of demand and relative costs of needed inputs or on the impact on the earth's ecosystem of certain technologies such as chemical fertilizers than on biological constraints inherent in the plants themselves. One must be careful of too closely evaluating present farm yields in any particular country or region in terms of experimental results or yields in other parts of the globe because of variations in rainfall, temperature, soil types, topography, or managerial abilities of farmers. It does appear, however, as though present yield levels are a long way from physiological limits.

A crop's photosynthetic efficiency, defined as the percentage of solar energy used relative to that available on a given land area, is the ultimate factor limiting crop output per acre. Actual position of leaves on plants, density of plant population, temperature, and plant physiology are key factors regulating photosynthetic efficiency. Increasing the upper yield limit can be accomplished by developing plants with greater photosynthetic efficiency or by improving cultural practices to improve efficiency per acre. Hybrid corn and sorghum plants as well as new varieties of wheat and rice plants are all more efficient users of solar energy, and their smaller size permits a dramatic gain in the number of plants per acre. Ultimately, the rate of increase for man's major food crops will begin to slow, but no one can say when with any certainty.

Even with the global mid-twentieth century area-to-yield transition, it was clear that advanced or modern farm technologies were confined mainly to the rich industrial countries and to plantation and export crops in the poor countries. This was unfortunate because in the decades following World War II, Malthusian forces were vigorously at work in the poor countries. The spread and impact of modern medicine and sanitation throughout the less-developed world reduced death rates. But birth rates did not diminish. As a consequence, population growth rates soared far above any ever experienced by the now-industrialized countries at any time in their history. Almost by definition, a poor country was one with a runaway population growth rate.

In several poor countries, growth rates moved well above 3 percent a year. A population enlarging at 3 percent yearly doubles within a generation and multiplies eighteenfold within a century. This Malthusian arithmetic frightened agriculturalists because there were no vast frontier areas of fertile, well-watered land that could quickly and cheaply be brought under the plow. Most densely populated poor countries, particularly in Asia, had run out of land without being able to generate a takeoff in yield per acre. In India and Pakistan, for example, grain yields had remained almost unchanged for six decades.

The demand for food spurred by accelerating population growth and modest rises in income was outstripping the production of food. The poor countries were losing the capacity to feed themselves, either to grow or buy food needed. Food deficits mounted, and food prices spiraled. Year by year through the mid-1960s, the poor countries were becoming more dependent on food imported from the United States under the $1.5 billion yearly food-aid program.

Food shortages existing in the poor countries did not mean that agriculture was performing poorly there. Food production was increasing almost as rapidly in the developing countries as in the developed countries, roughly 20 percent per decade. But population growth in the poor countries offset gains in food production, leaving little to satisfy increases in income. A comparison of Latin America and Western Europe illustrates this. Both increased food production around 2.5 to 3.0 percent per year during the decade before 1966. But in Europe, population was growing around 1 percent yearly, whereas in Latin America it was multiplying at almost 3 percent yearly. Diets in Europe were steadily upgraded, whereas in Latin America food output *per person* was declining.

123

*the area-to-
yield transition*

To make matters worse, the centrally planned economies of Eastern Europe and Asia, with few if any exceptions, were showing consistently poor agricultural performances as a result of lack of investment in agriculture, poor management, and meager incentives. During the 1960s, the Soviet Union and mainland China became grain importers, China at the rate of 5–6 million tons annually. And East Germany, once the breadbasket for all Germany, began to import increasingly larger quantities of feed and food grains.

Meanwhile in North America, a virtual explosion in food production was taking place. As a result of this and growing food deficits throughout much of the world, North America emerged as the breadbasket of the world.

Asia, Africa, and Latin America, which had each been net cereal exporters prior to World War II, shipping largely to Europe, had suddenly found that enlarged populations were consuming what had once been their exportable surpluses. By 1950, the poor countries were importing several million tons of grain each year, principally from North America. By 1960, this flow of food grains had increased to 13 million tons. In 1966, it reached a peak of 32 million tons, half of which consisted of food-aid shipments from the United States. By 1966, only North America and Australia remained grain exporters among the world's seven geographic regions. North America's grain exports were nearly 60 million tons.

Two consecutive monsoon failures, in 1965 and 1966, on the Indo-Pakistan subcontinent, a region of 625 million people, brought the adverse food–population trends into sharp focus. Had the United States been unable to meet the huge food needs in drought-stricken Asia, millions or tens of millions might have starved.

The situation was alarming. In 1966, the U.S. Department of Agriculture produced a chart, using a series of conservative assumptions regarding production prospects; it indicated that by 1985, the United States would no longer have the capacity to produce exportable surpluses sufficient to cover the food deficits anticipated in the poor countries. In 1967, the President's Science Advisory Commission report pointed out that during the first half of the 1960s, population in the poor countries was increasing at 2.5 percent a year, whereas food production was growing at only 1.6 percent. In short, food and population were on a collision course. Some observers were predicting massive famine in Asia by 1975.

At the time these gloomy projections were being made, six of the world's seven most populous countries were food-deficient: China, India, the Soviet Union, Indonesia, Pakistan, and Japan. Only the United States (the seventh) remained a net exporter of food. As a result of stagnating production in many developing countries and the monsoon failures in the Indo-Pakistan subcontinent, per capita food production in the less-developed countries had fallen for three consecutive years.

SUGGESTED READINGS

Brown, Lester R., *Increasing World Food Output*, Washington, D.C.: U.S. Government Printing Office, 1965.

Brown, Lester R., "The World Outlook for Conventional Agriculture," *Science*, November 3, 1967.

Cloud, Preston, "Mineral Resources from the Sea," in *Resources and Man*, Committee on Man, National Academy of Sciences–National Research Council, San Francisco: W.H. Freeman, 1969.

Food and Agriculture Organization of the United Nations, *The State of Food and Agriculture,* Rome: FAO, 1968.

Freeman, Orville, "Malthus, Marx and the North American Breadbasket," *Foreign Affairs*, July, 1967.

Paddock, William, and Paul Paddock, *Famine 1975: America's Decision, Who Will Survive,* Boston: Little, Brown, 1968.

10
agricultural breakthrough in the poor countries

Just when the world food situation looked dark-est in the mid-1960s, certain critical changes were occurring. Governments in many poor countries shifted emphasis from industrial to agricultural development. The United States adopted a tighter food-aid policy toward recipi-ent countries. And grain prices in the world marketplace soared. These changes combined to create a new political–economic climate in the hungry countries, a climate extremely favorable to agriculture.

Neglect of agriculture was widespread during the 1950s. Planners and politicians in the poor countries, and their advisers elsewhere, favored industry. They reasoned that economic devel-opment and modernization depended primarily on industrial growth. National policies and bud-gets, and much international technical and capi-tal assistance, were geared toward industrial development. Instead of strongly backing indigenous agricultural advance, politicians had grown accustomed to depending on food aid from abroad. This attitude is illustrated by the response of one Indian official who, when urged early in 1965 to build grain reserves as a hedge against famine, replied, "Why should we bother? Our reserves are the wheat fields of Kansas."

The inexorable pressure of population on land and available food supplies changed this attitude. The monsoon failures in southern Asia and the impending food crisis made political leaders in the poor countries suddenly and sharply aware both of the extent to which they had lost the capacity to feed themselves and the degree to which they had become dependent upon *one* external food source. Their food needs were being supplied by grain fields located in a single climatic region. American- and Canadian-grown crops are affected by the same weather cycle. What would result if natural disaster or disease were to hit North American agriculture? The close brush with famine became a critical turning point in global efforts to combat hunger.

Even before the monsoon failures, the United States had been urging countries receiving food aid to develop their own food reserves, but to little avail. By early 1965, the United States realized that the ready availability of its food aid had permitted agricultural neglect abroad, helping to bring on the food crisis. Massive food aid provided under Public Law 480 as a means of relieving hunger while simultaneously disposing of unwanted American surpluses alleviated both problems but solved neither. Long-term food-aid agreements of one to four years effectively postponed any meaningful decisions by recipient governments to improve agriculture. In some countries, food aid was actually aggravating the problem of hunger by depressing the prices of wheat and rice to the point where it was unprofitable for local farmers to use fertilizer. It was clear that a change in American policy was necessary.

Later in 1965, emphasis shifted away from direct food aid to helping countries increase their own food production. The United States adopted what was essentially a "short tether." Instead of allocating food aid in terms of years, as had been the practice, it became available for only two or three months at a time. Recipient countries were asked to take certain actions to improve agriculture, such as the building of fertilizer plants, farm-to-market roads, and the organization of farm credit systems. Renewal of food-aid agreements depended upon meeting these commitments. In particular, the United States encouraged both the formulation of more enlightened agricultural price policies and investment in rural infrastructure to make it profitable for farmers to use modern technology.

This policy change became feasible because U.S. surpluses had been reduced to desirable reserve levels. It became possible for the first time to strengthen the efforts of those politicians in the poor countries who were pressing for more action to increase local food-producing capacity. One minister of agriculture commented at the time, "Now I can get the Finance Minister to return my phone calls."

In conjunction with the short-tether policy, the United States increased financial assistance for agricultural development abroad, mainly to finance fertilizer shipments. At the same time, technical resources of American land-grant universities and the U.S. Department of Agriculture were more effectively mobilized.

New political commitments to agriculture occurred at the top levels of government in several developing countries. Prime Minister Demirel of Turkey, Presidents Ayub of Pakistan and Marcos of the Philippines, and Agriculture Minister Subramaniam of India gave strong personal backing to crop-production campaigns. Budgetary and foreign-exchange allocations to agriculture increased sharply. Prime Minister Maiwandwal of Afghanistan, for example, assessed each ministry 2.5 percent of its operating budget in the summer of 1966 to launch a crash wheat-production program. India allocated 20 percent of its foreign exchange to import fertilizer. Fertilizer supplies doubled or tripled in a score of countries between 1965 and 1970. In several countries, restrictions were lifted on importation of irrigation pumps. But perhaps most importantly, country after country adopted guaranteed prices at the farm level for wheat and rice.

Partly as a result of these policy changes in many poor countries and in the United States, the economic climate for agriculture was extraordinarily good from 1966 to 1968, probably better than at any other time in recent history. The short leash

128

man and his environment: food

on food aid helped to bolster grain prices within food-aid recipient countries. National price-support policies assured farmers of a floor to the market at harvest time, making it feasible for them to invest in fertilizer at planting time. And in addition to the effect of specific policies, a general scarcity of food grains in the world marketplace had caused grain prices to rise. The world rice price, always somewhat higher than that of wheat, climbed sharply in 1967 and 1968, soaring from its normal range of around $120 per ton to past $200 per ton. A ton of rice could be exchanged for three tons of wheat on the world market.

Into this greatly improved political–economic climate extraordinary new high-yielding varieties of wheat and rice were fortuitously introduced and rapidly diffused in several of the larger poor countries: India, Pakistan, the Philippines, Indonesia, Turkey, and Ceylon. The new varieties are the most exciting agricultural technology ever to be introduced into the developing countries. They are not just marginally better than traditional or indigenous strains. Plant breeders, following in the footsteps of Mendel and Luther Burbank (who created hybrid plants on his experimental farm in Sebastopol, California, in the late nineteenth and early twentieth centuries), have quietly produced, by painstakingly crossbreeding assorted cereal grains, new strains that actually double yields with proper management and sufficient water and fertilizer. These new seeds may affect the well-being of more people in a shorter period of time than any other technological advance in history.

The combination of a favorable economic climate and the propitious introduction of the new seeds resulted in an abrupt and surprising breakthrough in food production in the hungry countries in the late 1960s. Unprecedented increases in cereal harvests have been reported in country after country. Pakistan raised its wheat production 60 percent between 1967 and 1969, a most remarkable upward leap. India upped its wheat harvest by one-half from 1965 to 1969. The Philippines ended more than half a century of dependence on rice imports. Ceylon's rice harvest increased by a third in two years. Takeoffs in wheat yields per acre on the Indo-Pakistan subcontinent following the introduction of the new wheats make the earlier corn-yield takeoff in the United States or the rice-yield takeoff in Japan seem pedestrian by comparison (Figure 11). Other Asian countries using the new varieties include Turkey, Burma, Mayalsia, Indonesia, Vietnam, Iran, Afghanistan, Nepal, Laos, and probably mainland China. Known popularly as the *green revolution*, this agricultural breakthrough has measurably improved the prospects of feeding the increases in man's numbers and reducing the incidence of hunger on the planet.

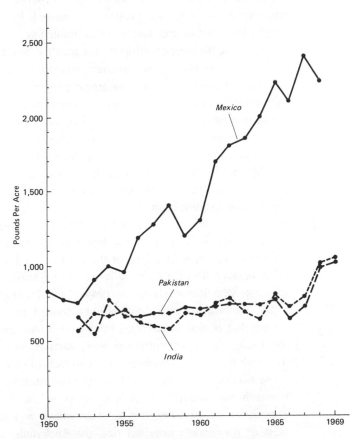

figure 11. *Wheat yields in Mexico, Pakistan, and India. (From Lester R. Brown. 1970.* Seeds of Change: The Green Revolution and Development in the 1970s. *New York: Praeger, and London: Pall Mall Press.) Used by permission.*

Heretofore, most advances in agricultural technology were geared to temperate-zone conditions or to plantation agriculture that at best benefited those living in tropical countries only residually. The new high-yielding wheats and rices are the product of the first systematic effort to develop agricultural technology designed specifically to take advantage of the unique natural growing conditions of the tropics and subtropics, particularly their wealth of solar energy, and to improve the lot of millions who live in desperate material poverty. The twentieth-century agricultural revolution that first occurred in the temperate northern countries is now, through these new varieties and associated technologies, spreading to and affecting the poor countries to the south, where two-thirds of mankind reside. Many southern countries are currently making the transition from the area-expanding to the yield-increasing method of enlarging food production.

The new wheats came first. They were developed in Mexico by the Rockefeller Foundation (in collaboration with the Mexican government). In 1941, Mexico appealed to the Rockefeller Foundation for help with agricultural development. This was before the birth of the United Nations and its Food and Agriculture Organization (FAO) and before the numerous technical-assistance agencies. After conducting an exploratory survey, a pioneering program was begun under the direction of George Harrar, now president of the Rockefeller Foundation. Plant breeder Norman E. Borlaug was among three American scientists who joined Harrar in 1944. Over the next two decades, Borlaug and his collaborators created new Mexican wheats that tripled wheat production in that country and that are revolutionizing agriculture in many parts of the world. For this work Borlaug was awarded the 1970 Nobel Peace Prize.

The new rices have come largely from the International Rice Research Institute (IRRI) at Los Banos in the Philippines. Encouraged by the success of Mexican wheats and aware that most of the world's poor eat rice, the Rockefeller and Ford Foundations jointly founded IRRI in 1962. Some 10,000 strains of rice from every corner of the world were collected, providing plant breeders with a huge bank of genetic raw materials from which to create, in engineering fashion, better rice. Following methods developed in the Mexican program, scientists met success early with IR-8, called *miracle rice*, the most productive of the new rices. IR-8 is a cross between Dee-geo-woo-gen, a dwarf rice from Taiwan, and Peta, a tall, high-yielding, and disease-resistant variety from Indonesia.

In the tropics, traditional cereal varieties are the result of millennia of natural selection. Strains that survived are those capable of competing with weeds for sunlight and withstanding heavy tropical rain and floods. The result has been tall, thin plants able to keep their heads above water and in the sunlight. These traditional plants are not highly responsive to fertilizer. When fertilized liberally, the plants become top-heavy with grain and fall over, or *lodge*, before the grain is ripe, causing heavy losses.

The key to the productivity of the new varieties is a remarkable feat of biological engineering that greatly enhances their responsiveness to fertilizer. Plant breeders redesigned the wheat and rice plants, producing plants with short, stiff stems that stand up under the weight of heavier yields. The old long-strawed varieties were able to absorb only about 40 lb of nitrogen per acre before yields began to decline as a result of lodging. Yields from the new dwarf wheat and rice varieties increase until the nitrogen application reaches 120 lb per acre.

The new varieties not only respond to much larger quantities of fertilizer; they also use fertilizer more efficiently. A pound of nitrogen applied to traditional cereals raised yields about 10 lb. A pound applied to the new plants usually produces 15–20 lb of additional grain. Thus, a given level of production can be reached with the new seeds using far less fertilizer. The new plants are, in fact, more efficient users of water, land, and labor as well as fertilizer.

In addition to being more responsive to fertilizer, the new strains are aseasonal, that is, not very sensitive to variations in photoperiod (the average number of hours of light per day). This gives them great adaptability to a wide range of differing geographical locations and seasons of the year. Through millennia of selection, traditional varieties in given locales are very sensitive to daylength. They have become responsive to, and dependent upon, specific seasonal cycles and can be planted only at a certain time of the year, for example, at the onset of the monsoon season for rice.

Using germ plasm from widely scattered parts of the world gave the new varieties cosmopolitan parentage that helped to reduce their photoperiod sensitivity. Borlaug, for example, used wheats from Japan, the United States, Australia, and Colombia in the Mexican breeding program. In addition, he alternated growing sites, raising a summer crop just south of the U.S. border, and a winter crop near Mexico City, some 800 miles away. The two sites differed in daylength and other environmental factors. Mexican wheats today flourish from Turkey and Canada in the north to Argentina in the South. This adaptability is something new.

Many of the new varieties also mature early. IR-8, for example, is ready for harvest in four months. Local varieties take five or six.

As a result of their high-yield capacity, the new grains have spread like prairie fire in the poor countries where ecological conditions are suited to their use. So dramatic are the harvests that they easily convince tradition-bound farmers to adopt the new seeds and the necessary modern farming practices. In Asia, the area planted to high-yielding cereals in the 1964–1965 crop year was estimated at 200 acres, and that largely for experimental and industrial purposes; the next year, there were 41,000 acres; then 4 million; then 16 million; then 31 million; and in 1969–1970, the total reached 44 million acres. This is close to one-tenth of the cereal-producing land in Asia (excluding mainland China). Almost one-tenth of India's cereal acreages now have the new strains.

The poor countries have been able to import the new wheats by the shipload at prices only marginally higher than the world market prices. Since many countries were already importing cereals, the new technology was essentially free, sparing them large research and development costs. And because the seeds could be imported in huge quantities, the time required to multiply new seed was drastically condensed. Pakistan, for

agricultural
breakthrough
in the poor
countries

example, imported 42,000 tons of new Mexican wheat seeds in 1967, enough to plant more than a million acres. Harvest from this crop provided enough to cover all Pakistan's wheatland, compressing into two years a process that would normally take many years.

But perhaps even more important than the actual tonnage of dwarf wheats and rices imported are the prototype they represent and the genetic raw materials they provide. Already local plant breeders are refining and modifying the prototype to specifically suit local growing conditions and tastes, cross-breeding imported and local strains to create newer varieties with desired characteristics. Two promising rices released in East India in 1969 are Jaya and Padma, both local variations of the dwarf prototype. Other local modifications are being released in Ceylon, Malaysia, and Thailand. Local improvements on the dwarf wheat prototype are already in widespread use in India and Pakistan.

Farmers in the poor countries are increasingly viewing the future in terms of new seeds and new techniques. When Filipino Farmer of the Year, 58-year-old Andres de la Cruz, was asked what variety of rice he was going to plant next season, he answered, "I don't know. I'm still waiting for a newer variety."

The agricultural breakthrough is wonderful, but it has far to go. It has not yet been achieved in all poor countries. And it is thus far confined principally to wheat and rice crops and to geographical areas with adequate water supplies in the case of wheat and adequate, controlled water in the case of rice. The dwarf wheats yield best under high-rainfall or irrigated conditions. The dwarf rices do not perform well in conditions of natural flooding or in rain-fed fields, where they may be submerged for some time. Water, in short, is the chief ecological factor affecting the spread of the new varieties. But even with these constraints, the deteriorating food situation has been arrested in some of the most populous countries of Asia: India, Pakistan, Indonesia, and the Philippines.

Plant breeders are working to develop wheats that will yield abundantly under low-rainfall conditions and high-yield rices that are more tolerant of flooding. Farmers and governments are expanding and intensifying irrigation and flood-control systems. Efforts are also under way in developing high-yielding varieties of corn, sorghum, millet, potatoes, and legumes.

The rapid and unprecedented rates of crop-yield increases noted above cannot be maintained in Asia over an extended period. An important reason is that most of Asia's intensively irrigated and most fertile farmland, land producing a disproportionate share of the region's food, has already been planted to the new varieties. As the initial impact of the new seeds begins to subside, it is likely that year-to-year gains will be slowed. But the upward trend is likely to continue for some time, barring war or internal political disintegration, because there are substantial opportunities for further increases in yields in these countries. For example, rice yields have been climbing for seven decades in Japan; and corn yields, for three decades in the United States.

Among numerous sources of increases in yields remaining to be exploited are a continuing increase in the area planted to high-yielding varieties, in the quantity of fertilizer available, in investment in flood-control and irrigation facilities (especially tubewells and pumps), in the mechanization of operations that contribute to high yields (such as seedbed preparation), and in the adoption of still more efficient high-yielding varieties that are now on the drawing boards.

multiple cropping

The genetic characteristics of the new varieties offer many fresh possibilities for multiple cropping in tropical–subtropical regions where water supplies are adequate. With reduced sensitivity to daylength and early maturity, many new strains can be planted throughout the year in a variety of cropping patterns; and their high-yield potential provides a strong incentive for multiple cropping.

In the tropics, lack of water during the dry season and an inability to maintain soil fertility have traditionally limited multiple cropping. Now, with expanding availability of chemical fertilizer, continuing development of water resources, and use of crops with lower water requirements (such as wheat or sorghum) during the dry season, these constraints are being overcome. Where water supplies are assured and where fertilizer is available, farming throughout the year with two, three, and occasionally even four crops of the same grain or various combinations is becoming feasible. Thousands of farmers in northern India are now alternating a crop of early maturing wheat grown during the dry, sunny winter season with rice raised during the rainy summer season. Scientists at Los Banos in the Philippines regularly harvest three crops of rice per year. In Mysore, India, farmers are now producing three crops of corn every fourteen months, using intensive applications of irrigation water and fertilizer.

Expanding farming into the dry season allows far more of the abundant solar energy of southern countries to be converted into food. Data from Indonesia and the Philippines show higher yields in the dry season than in the wet season for four high-yielding varieties grown at several different sites. Although environmental conditions varied widely among the sites, dry-season yields were consistently higher, averaging 52 percent above wet-season yields.

The economic advantages of farming during the dry season are obvious. Increased utilization of farm labor, draft animals, and farm equipment that formerly lay idle during the dry season, combined with higher yields per unit of land, water, fertilizer, and labor with the new varieties, make dry-season cropping exceedingly profitable. Because substantially higher profits are now possible, investment is justified in dry-season irrigation facilities, such as tubewells or water-impounding structures, that may not be financially attractive with older varieties.

Man's knowledge of multiple cropping in the tropics is still in its infancy. Its great potential for increasing the productivity of land is just beginning to be exploited. But producing two or more crops a year is not an unmixed blessing. It sometimes strains the agricultural ecosystem by creating minor soil deficiencies and special pest and disease problems. There may also be special problems of water management and in some cases the unique problem of harvesting and drying grain while the monsoon is in full sway.

Nevertheless, the new varieties and multiple cropping are changing the concept of agricultural productivity. The ancients measured productivity in terms of grain returned for grain planted. Today, in a temperate zone country like the United States, agricultural productivity is measured in terms of yield per acre per crop, for example, 75 bushels of corn per acre per crop. But in the tropics, with the new technologies, the measure is not how many bushels or tons per acre per crop, but how many bushels or tons per acre per year. Heretofore, farmers in much of Asia harvested scarcely half a ton of grain per year; now many are producing several times that amount. Triple-cropping rice at Los Banos has yielded eight tons of grain per acre per year.

More and more, man in the tropics and subtropics is producing food on land that traditionally lay idle during the dry season. As multiple cropping and year-round farming spread, they are profoundly altering the way of life of the countryside, divorcing it from the traditional seasonal crop cycle that dictated not only planting and harvesting times but the timing of religious festivals, weddings, and a host of other social events as well.

engines of change

The word *revolution* is used frequently and is greatly abused, but no other word adequately describes the effects of the new plant varieties on the poor countries. Increased cereal production (and its potential effect on hunger and nutrition) is just one aspect of the agricultural breakthrough. Agricultural scientists have achieved a technological breakthrough that foreshadows widespread economic, political, social, and cultural changes throughout the developing world, promising to affect every segment of society. Wherever the new seeds are used, they are becoming engines of change because farmers and societies must adopt new practices to exploit them. They may be to the agricultural revolution in Asia and elsewhere what the steam engine was to the Industrial Revolution in Europe.

And the effects will not be limited to the poor countries. Already the high-yielding plants are permanently altering the global pattern of agricultural production, reordering long-standing patterns of international trade in cereals, and reducing the need for U.S. food aid.

Major changes like the ones occurring in the poor countries today are not lived through without problems and strains. The new varieties are being introduced on a massive scale in many societies still practicing agriculture essentially as it was practiced in Biblical times. Technological progress that other nations experienced over centuries is being compressed into decades and, in some cases, into years. There are many second-generation problems associated with the current agricultural breakthrough, problems of success and change that may cause the agricultural revolution to lose some of its momentum. Awareness of such problems prompted one writer to ask whether the green revolution was a cornucopia or a Pandora's box. But awareness of the problems may help to steer the course of the revolution and generalize its benefits.

marketing

The most immediate and visible obstacle to the agriculture revolution is the woefully inadequate state of marketing systems in countries where the new varieties are being planted. With the new technologies, farmers' marketable surpluses of cereals have increased far faster, proportionately, than production. A farmer who is accustomed to marketing a fifth of his wheat harvest finds his marketable surplus triples when his crop suddenly increases 40 percent. Even after retaining more for family consumption, as many are doing, farmers who have doubled their output with the new seeds are increasing their marketable surpluses severalfold.

The green revolution found some countries with marketing systems oriented primarily toward handling imported grain. Over the past two decades, many great Asian coastal cities turned more to their harbors for food than to their own countrysides. Cities like Calcutta, Bombay, Karachi, Madras, and Djakarta have lived literally from ship-to-mouth for extended periods on wheat sent under the U.S. food-aid program. Marketable surpluses produced in the countryside had diminished and were not even beginning to meet the food needs of the large cities. Consequently, systems designed to move food surpluses from countryside to cities or other food-deficit areas have atrophied from disuse.

Now domestic marketable surpluses are threatening to overwhelm all components of the marketing system: storage, transport, grading and processing operations, and the local intelligence system. Storage facilities, seldom needed in the past, have been so inadequate that great amounts of grain have had to be stored in open fields or in public buildings such as schoolhouses. During April and May of 1968 scores of village schools closed in northern India because the buildings were needed to handle the overflow wheat crop. They were the only uninhabited buildings capable of storing a record crop of wheat that had already overwhelmed all other local storage facilities. When the classrooms were filled to the ceiling and the grain was still coming in from the fields, it was stored in the open. Fortunately, the rains were late, and the exposed grain was finally safely loaded in boxcars. The bumper crop was 35 percent higher than the previous record crop. In West Pakistan, land planted to the new IR-8 rice rose from 10,000 acres to nearly a million in one year (1967–1968). West Pakistan suddenly found itself with a sizable exportable surplus of rice, but without the processing, transport, and pricing facilities needed to handle export trade efficiently.

The agricultural gaps between the rich and poor countries now seem far greater in marketing than in production. A comparison of grain-marketing techniques in India and the United States demonstrates this. In India, where grain changes hands in small quantities, the farmer and the local grain merchant usually meet each other face to face for the initial transaction. The buyer personally smells, feels, and sometimes even tastes the grain. Negotiations are often prolonged and usually center around a transaction of perhaps four sacks of wheat. All of this is very different from marketing in the United States, where vast quantities of grain are bought and sold without being seen by either the buyer or the seller. Transactions are often on paper only. Buying and selling grain resembles to a large degree the buying and selling of stocks on the exchanges. As grain leaves the farm in the United States, it is scientifically graded for cleanliness or percentage of foreign material, moisture content, and protein content. Then the grain is classified according to detailed government specifications. And on the basis of this classification, it moves through the marketing system. Only with grades and standards that buyers and sellers have confidence in and adhere to is this level of efficiency possible.

Antiquated marketing procedures must be revolutionized to keep pace with the new challenge of increased production. Actual and threatened grain losses due to inadequate marketing systems are drawing attention to the imbalance between resources devoted to production and to marketing. Since 1960, some development-assistance organizations have attempted to improve domestic marketing in the developing countries, but it has been a slow and tedious process. Much more investment will be needed in all components of the marketing system.

disease

Whenever exogenous varieties are introduced on a large scale, as with the new wheats and rices, farmers must be constantly alert to the threat of plant disease. The classic example is the destruction of the Irish potato crop by blight in the late 1840s. As pointed out in Chapter 1, Ireland's population dropped by half as a result of famine and subsequent emigration, late marriages, and low birth rates.

The potato does not readily contract blight. Temperature and humidity, among other factors, have to be exactly right— or, rather, wrong. But when these very specific conditions occur, the crop failure can be fatal. The same is true of wheat rust and some other diseases attacking cereals. The resistance of the new wheats and rices to disease strains of their new habitats has not been thoroughly tested. Since a major share of the acreage in Asia devoted to high-yielding cereals is planted to exogenous varieties, the disease threat deserves close surveillance. The new wheats developed in Mexico are rather resistant to the wheat rusts currently prevalent in Mexico, but not necessarily to those found on the far side of the globe.

Rice seems to be more plagued by disease than wheat is. In part, this is because rice is almost always grown in a warmer, moister environment that is more conducive to the spread of diseases. In order to achieve optimum yields with the new varieties, the density of the plant population is invariably increased. Combined with much heavier fertilization that brings with it lush vegetative growth, the "crowding" creates ideal conditions for plant epidemics and infestation of pests, as it does in human societies. The dominant disease of rice in Asia is rice blast, a disease occurring more frequently as the use of nitrogen fertilizer and the density of the vegetation increase.

Although the threat of rice disease is a real one, there is much more preventive technology in the research bank now than there was when the potato blight hit Ireland. As the exogenous varieties are crossed with local ones, the risk of an outbreak of disease on that scale is reduced. At the same time, a greater number of new varieties are being used, and sources of germ plasm are becoming more diverse.

consumer resistance

Another second-generation problem is consumer resistance to the unfamiliar appearance, taste, or consistency of new grains. New varieties are rarely as acceptable at first as traditional varieties to which people are accustomed. Cooking qualities of IR-8 rice, for example, cause it to be less popular than local varieties in many areas of Asia. The new rice is more chalky and brittle, yielding more broken grains during milling. As for wheat, the Mexican varieties are predominantly red; Indians and Pakistanis prefer amber wheats.

Plant breeders are working to cross the new varieties with local strains. Crosses often eliminate less-desirable characteristics, developing instead the taste, cooking, and milling properties that suit local preference. Meanwhile, lower prices make the grain attractive to some groups, and consumer tastes change or adapt over time.

scarce credit and foreign exchange

Large-scale farmers who are able to finance their own purchases initially have the advantage over small-scale farmers in acquiring farm inputs needed for modernizing agriculture. The rate at which small-scale farmers adopt new technologies is determined frequently by the availability of farm credit on terms they can afford. If, like the great majority of Asian farmers, they are dependent on the local money lender, whose interest rates often range from 20 to 100 percent per year, they may find it prohibitive to use modern inputs such as fertilizer.

One of the great ironies of the agricultural breakthrough is that achieving self-sufficiency in food may create a more serious foreign-exchange crisis than continued dependence on food aid from abroad would have done. Because food aid comes in kind not in money, the savings in American food aid, for example, cannot be used to buy the increased amounts of fertilizer and other farm inputs needed to use the seeds effectively. Only the United States and the Soviet Union are fortunate enough to have within their borders commercial deposits of all raw material necessary for a modern fertilizer industry: phosphate rock, potash, sulfur, and petroleum or natural gas. Most countries must import at least a portion of their fertilizer raw material. Some, such as India and Thailand, must import nearly all.

distributing the benefits

Perhaps the most compelling, unsettling, and far-reaching of the consequences inherent in the agricultural breakthrough is that of distributing the gains and benefits of the new technologies. The new varieties not only double the level of production over the levels achieved with local varieties, but, in doing so, they often triple or quadruple profits. Millions of large and small farmers, suddenly earning incomes they had not dreamed possible, are already benefiting from the breakthrough. The aspirations of millions of others, especially landless rural laborers, are being aroused in the process. As the new varieties and the new technologies associated with them spread, they introduce rapid and sweeping changes, creating a wave of expectations throughout society and placing great pressure on the existing social order and political systems.

Conflicts have already arisen, and are bound to continue to arise, between landowners and tenants, between both of these groups and laborers who have no land, and even between groups of landless laborers. In Tanjore, one of India's model agricultural-development districts, forty-two persons were burned to death during December, 1968, when two groups of landless laborers clashed tragically. They were fighting over the best way to gain a share of benefits from the new varieties used by the district's landowners. One group wanted to enforce a boycott against farmers using the new seeds until landlords raised wages; the other group was willing to accept prevailing wages.

Among landed farmers themselves, distribution of the gains from the new technologies is very uneven. A new "rich" class of farmers is bound to arise, made up of those with adequate water, proximity to markets, and access to fertilizer. Where capital is required to purchase essential inputs, larger farms will have the advantage. But where labor is the critical or required input, smaller family farms may fare better than large farms that depend heavily on hired labor. There is hope that a new entrepreneurial class will emerge as a result of greatly expanded opportunities in agribusiness. But others will be left behind, and many who have had positions of wealth and power will lose those positions.

Regional disparities often resulting from ecological factors will become particularly acute as the new varieties spread, because water is the dominant factor determining whether or not the new grains can be successfully adopted. In Turkey, farmers along the well-watered and fertile coastal plain are benefiting much more from the new wheats than farmers situated on the arid Anatolian plateau. West Pakistan's success with the new varieties is far greater than East Pakistan's, where ecological factors are not suited to them. West Pakistan, an area of low rainfall, was ideally prepared for the new varieties, since nearly all cropland is irrigated; and considerable effort has been made to exploit underground water resources through tubewells and pumps. In East Pakistan, one of the world's heaviest-rainfall areas, spread of the new varieties has proceeded at a snail's pace because of lack of water control and effective irrigation. The new varieties have transformed West Pakistan from a region of acute scarcity and heavy imports to one of surpluses and unprecedented prosperity. But East Pakistan continues to be a food-deficit area, hard-pressed to keep food production abreast of population growth. Political difficulties associated with this situation helped to undermine President Ayub Khan's authority in 1968, leading to a period of continuing political turmoil in Pakistan in the early 1970s.

In its most basic form, the question of who benefits must be considered in terms of farmers and consumers. As the new technologies heighten expectations among farmers and city dwellers alike, food prices are certain to become an increasingly important issue. Agricultural price policy strongly affects the nature and direction of agricultural development. It determines, among other things, how the benefits of progress are to be shared between the cities and the countryside.

If price supports are set too high, they may provide production incentives and higher incomes to farmers but at the same time create discontent among city dwellers whose food costs rise. If supports are set too low, consumers will gain most of the benefits but farmers may be unable to afford inputs needed to exploit the new grains. Fortunately, the countryside has been the principal beneficiary over the past few years. As long as food scarcity prevails, farmers will probably continue to reap most of the benefits. But as food production expands and a country approaches or reaches self-sufficiency, prices will be depressed unless markets are gained abroad. Lower prices would make consumers the principal beneficiaries of the new efficiencies. Finding the right price level and other means of distributing the benefits equitably among diverse social groups is one of the challenges issuing from the agricultural revolution in the poor countries.

self-sufficiency

The agricultural breakthrough is taking many nations long dependent on food imports to the point of self-sufficiency in local cereals, and in several cases it is generating exportable surpluses. The Philippines, first to use the new rices on a commercial basis, is now a net exporter. West Pakistan was a net exporter of both wheat and rice in 1969 and 1970. Mexico has recently exported small quantities of wheat, corn, and rice. India, with its 540 million inhabitants, expects to be self-sufficient in wheat and rice by 1972. Kenya, Brazil, and Thailand are all exporters of corn. Turkey is expected to reach self-sufficiency in wheat soon.

Who will buy the exportable surpluses that some poor countries are now generating and that others will eventually produce? The success and continuation of the green revolution depends greatly on the availability of foreign markets. If poor countries are to fully exploit the new agricultural technologies to meet food needs and to speed economic growth, they will have to gain access to the markets of rich countries.

Rapid gains in cereal production are usually much easier as long as a country is a deficit producer. Under these circumstances, it can set domestic prices independently of world prices, focusing on the price level needed to provide the necessary incentive. Once a country reaches self-sufficiency, however, and begins to produce exportable supluses, it must then be sure its prices are below world prices or be prepared to subsidize exports.

In several Asian countries, expanding grain production following years of scarcity is already pushing prices downward. In some countries, prices are resting at the government-support level. The Philippine Rice and Corn Production Coordinating Council, the country's price-supporting agency, used up so much of its funds buying rice at high prices in 1968 that it had only limited funds with which to support the 1969 crop. The

council's rice is the first exportable surplus from the Philippines in more than half a century. But with the continuing
decline in world prices, it can be exported only at substantial
loss. Should government resources not be adequate to maintain support prices, agricultural progress In the Philippines
could be set back seriously.

This pattern could be repeated in many countries as cereal
production surges ahead. Several countries now in a position
to export, or fast approaching that postion—including, in addition to the Philippines, Mexico (wheat), Kenya (corn), and
Pakistan (wheat)—are facing grave problems because internal
prices are higher than the world market price.

Rich countries, with their modern agricultural economies
built on protection, as in Western Europe or Japan, or dependent on exports, as is the United States, face the threat of a
serious decline in world cereal prices. They are beginning to
realize that planning must start now for a global pattern of
agricultural production during the seventies that will be very
different from the pattern which existed in the sixties. But at
present, the rich countries do not seem eager to modify their
protectionist policies and welcome the poor countries into
world grain markets.

It should be pointed out that exportable surpluses in the
poor countries are economic surpluses that domestic markets
cannot absorb. Their existence does not mean that diets have
become adequate and populations well fed. Only over the
longer run, as incomes continue to rise and/or as prices begin
to decline, are diets substantially affected. But the agricultural
breakthrough offers the potential for higher incomes and more
and better food for millions.

That the modern breakthrough in agricultural production
has a direct bearing on potential improvements in diet and
income can be seen from the experiences of Mexico, where the
green revolution is the most advanced. From 1900 to 1940,
Mexico's agriculture was stagnant; daily caloric intake per person was an estimated 1800 calories. Agriculture began to grow
rapidly in the 1940s, averaging more than 5 percent a year
between 1940 and 1960; the economy as a whole grew at an

annual rate of 6 percent. As a result of this rapid and sustained growth in both food production and purchasing power, daily caloric intake in Mexico increased from 1800 to 2650 calories per person, an increase of nearly 50 percent in twenty years. This does not mean that all Mexicans are well nourished today. A large segment of the population, mainly the rural poor in southern Mexico, has been bypassed by the new technologies. But the average food-energy intake in the country is now well above the minimum established by nutritionists, and this in spite of very rapid population growth.

In Mexico, per capita cereal production rose from 495 to 680 pounds during the 1960s. Even with more people and greater food-purchasing power, the domestic demand within Mexico has not kept pace with supply. Agricultural prices have declined by about 1 percent a year over a twenty-year period, and Mexico has sought export markets for its surpluses: mainly cereals, fruits, and vegetables. Still in its early stages, the green revolution has had a pronounced effect on per capita cereal production in several other important countries such as India, Pakistan, and Ceylon (Table 4).

Reaching self-sufficiency in cereal production permits a country to diversify land use, pouring resources formerly devoted to producing food grains into other crops and livestock. When foreign markets cannot be found for surplus cereals, because the products are not competitive in price or in quality, poor countries are forced to turn to agricultural diversification.

The new strains are facilitating diversification because they boost possibilities for multiple cropping. Short-season crops of vegetables and pulses can be sown between rice and wheat crops when there is an adequate supply of controlled water. The range of fruits and vegetables that can be produced in the tropical–subtropical regions is generally much greater than that in the temperate zones.

Diversification can be aimed at either the home market or the export market. As incomes rise in both poor and rich countries, and as people reach out for more varied diets, there will be steadily growing markets for fruits and vegetables, many of which can be included in a multiple-cropping regimen.

breakthrough
in the poor
countries

table 4
impact of production using new seeds
(annual production of selected cereals in countries
using new seeds)[a]

	India wheat	Pakistan wheat	Ceylon rice	Mexico all cereals
1960	53	87	201	495
1961	55	83	196	496
1962	59	87	213	525
1963	51	86	218	546
1964	46	83	213	611
1965	56	90	150	639
1966	46	71	188	649
1967	49	80	216	655
1968	76	116	247	680
1969	80	121	na	na

[a]Given in pounds per person of total population.
Source: U.S. Department of Agriculture.

Japan's removal of restrictions on banana imports in 1963 created new banana-export industries in nearby East Asian countries.

Jumbo jets and other modern transport are expanding possibilities for exporting fresh fruits and vegetables. Numerous high-value products, such as strawberries and lettuce, are now being flown several thousand miles from producer to market. New highways, the Friendship Highway in Thailand, for example, are linking areas of potential production with world markets. The newly paved road that passes through Afghanistan and the Khyber Pass, linking Pakistan with the Soviet Union and the Middle East, is opening an entirely new market for Pakistani farmers. The Soviet Union could become an important outlet for Pakistan's winter fruits and vegetables, much as the United States is for Mexico. Tropical–subtropical countries, with their year-round growing conditions, can complement the production patterns of the industrial northern countries, especially during the winter season.

As countries using the new seeds reach self-sufficiency in food grains, feed grains acquire a new status. Once per capita cereal production rises above 400 pounds, the additional grain produced is fed largely to animals. The expanding availability of low-cost grains, plus a continuing spread of modern poultry- and livestock-production technologies, make a poultry–livestock boom almost certain. How quickly this comes about depends on whether governments can effectively combine economic policies and new technologies as they did to stimulate cereal production.

Post–World War II broiler-production technologies developed in the United States are adaptable throughout the world with minimal modification. For the poor countries, husbanding poultry has several advantages over husbanding livestock. With modern techniques, grain-fed poultry costs less than grain-fed pork or beef, since feed requirements per pound are much lower. A well-managed broiler flock requires only 3 lb of grain per pound of meat produced, compared with an estimated 4 lb of grain per pound of pork and 7 lb for a pound of beef. Poultry need relatively little living space and have a short payout period. Chicks hatch in only twenty-one days and can be ready to market within ten to twelve weeks. Since chickens are small and can be consumed shortly after slaughter, they are easier to market in areas without refrigeration than pork or beef.

Intensive methods of broiler production are currently spreading and allowing poor countries to take advantage of modern technologies almost overnight. How rapidly poultry production expands in a given country is influenced by the growth of hatcheries producing high-quality chicks, the availability of poultry pharmaceuticals, the expansion of the feed-mixing industry, and consumer demand.

Normally, new broiler enterprises locate near large cities such as Bangkok, Istanbul, Rio de Janeiro, and São Paulo. Over time, as the number of consumers who can afford poultry multiplies, modern broiler production spreads from the outskirts of larger cities to smaller ones and subsequently to towns and villages. Countries such as Colombia, Thailand, Taiwan, and Turkey, which have growing urban middle classes, are witnessing dramatic expansions in poultry production.

Relative to poultry, expanding livestock production is much more difficult because the life cycle is longer, because improving pasture and acquiring better breeding stock are time-consuming activities, and because storage and preservation of meats is costly. But rising incomes and expanding export opportunities are stimulating the enlargement of livestock herds. There are regions of the world where conditions for such expansion are favorable. In parts of sub-Saharan Africa and Latin America, land is still abundant compared with densely populated Asia and North Africa. Substantial World Bank and Inter-American Development Bank loans are assisting efforts to develop the livestock potential there.

summary

To date, the greatest gains from the agricultural breakthrough are concentrated in Asia. But countries elsewhere are beginning to capitalize on the new seeds. Mexican wheats have been introduced in North Africa and are beginning to spread in Morocco and Tunisia. Libya and Algeria imported large supplies of the new wheat seeds in 1969. The Ivory Coast in West Africa more than doubled rice production during the 1960s. In Mexico, virtually all the wheatland is covered by the new varieties. Brazil and Paraguay gained dramatically in wheat production in 1968. But elsewhere in Latin America, neither the new wheats nor the new rices have made much progress. This is lamentable, since Latin America has relatively abundant water and land.

There is no agronomic reason why people in any developing country should be deprived of the benefits of the green revolution. High-yielding cereal varieties exist that are adaptable to almost every ecologic zone in the tropics and subtropics, and more are coming. The spread of the green revolution depends primarily not on technology, but on the commitment of political leadership to foster it and generalize its benefits. How rapidly the green revolution progresses also depends on the extent of financial and technical assistance from the rich countries. For example, many poor countries are not able to finance imports of as much fertilizer as they need.

However exciting and encouraging in the short run, the current wave of yield takeoffs should not reduce concern over the population problem. The green revolution is clearly not an ultimate solution to the food-population problem. The collision between population growth and food production has been averted only temporarily. But the agricultural breakthrough is buying urgently needed time, perhaps another decade or two, in which to stabilize population growth.

SUGGESTED READINGS

Asian Development Bank, *Asian Agricultural Survey*, Tokyo: University of Tokyo Press, 1969; Seattle: University of Washington Press, 1969.

Brown, Lester R., "Breakthrough Against Hunger," *Science Year*, Chicago: Field Enterprises, 1969.

Brown, Lester R., *Seeds of Change*, New York: Praeger, 1970.

Dalrymple, Dana, *Imports and Plantings of High-Yielding Varieties of Wheat and Rice in the Less Developed Nations*, Foreign Economic Development Service, U.S. Department of Agriculture, 1971.

Stakman, E. C., Richard Bradfield, and Paul C. Mangelsdorf, *Campaigns Against Hunger*, Cambridge 5, Mass.: Harvard University Press, Belknap Press, 1967.

Wharton, Clifton R., Jr., "The Green Revolution—Cornucopia or Pandora's Box?" *Foreign Affairs*, April, 1969.

11
new
food
technologies

Future food demands resulting from both population growth and rising incomes will be enormous. But developments in food technology promise to offset at least a small fraction of these demands. A revolution in food technology, quieter than the green revolution in conventional agricultural production, is underway.

In considering future food requirements, it is necessary to keep in mind the two sources of additional demand for food. Projecting food demands on the basis of population growth alone assumes that future populations will be not better or worse fed than at present. But virtually every country in the world, regardless of development level or ideology, is aiming at raising per capita income. Rising incomes, if realized, will greatly increase claims on the world's agricultural resources over and above those claims that will result from population growth alone. In Japan and many Western European countries, rising incomes are generating more growth in the demand for food than population increase is.

The way in which rising incomes affect mankind's food needs is perhaps best illustrated by looking at the grain required to feed high-

income and low-income populations at current dietary levels
(see Figure 12). Grain, it will be recalled, is a good indicator of
man's food requirements, since grain constitutes 53 percent of
what man eats when it is consumed directly and a large portion of the rest of man's diet when it is consumed indirectly in
the form of meat, milk, and eggs.

Today the 2 billion or more people living in the poor countries have available to them a yearly average of about 400 lb of
grain per person. Of this, around 10 percent is used for seed
for next year's crop, leaving 360 lb, or about 1 lb a day, for
actual consumption. Nearly all this must be consumed directly
simply to meet minimal energy requirements and to keep body
and soul together.

figure 12. *Income and per capita grain consumption. (From U.S. Department of Agriculture.)*

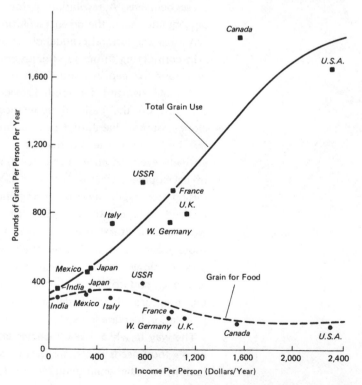

As incomes rise, the amount of grain per person that is consumed directly declines, however, leveling off at about 150 lb. More and more cereal grains are fed to livestock. But total grain used per person climbs steadily, eventually approaching a ton of grain per person each year, as in North America. The great bulk of this grain is consumed indirectly in the form of meat, milk, and eggs. This high consumption of livestock products places enormous claims on agricultural resources. The claims exerted against the earth's food-producing capacity by those living in the richest countries, say the United States or Canada, are perhaps four times as great as claims by those living in the poor countries. This can be expressed figuratively, in shorthand, in terms of a *grain-requirements ladder* (see Figure 13).

Historically, diets improved significantly only when grain supplies began to exceed direct-consumption needs, leaving large quantities to be converted into high-protein livestock products. But improving diets via this conventional route is both time consuming and costly. Livestock are rather inefficient in their conversion of plant materials into animal protein and fat products. They return to man only part of their energy intake in the form of edible food products. The rest is used to grow, to keep warm, to move, to reproduce. As a rule of thumb, it takes 7 lb of grain to produce 1 lb of beef, 4 lb of grain to produce 1 lb of pork, and 3 lb of grain to yield 1 lb of poultry, making poultry the most efficient converters.

Finding shortcuts to the costly livestock route to high-quality protein and fats is urgent in today's world and has caught the imagination of food technologists and other scientists: plant breeders, biochemists, and microbiologists. Scientists are now producing simulated livestock products based on plant materials that replace familiar meats, milk, and fats; creating entirely new vegetable-protein foods as substitutes for animal-protein products; breeding cereals with improved protein content; fortifying foods (particularly cereals) with synthetic amino acids; and exploring unusual new sources of protein.

If shortcuts to the livestock route to varied and nutritious diets become widely available and acceptable, the claims on

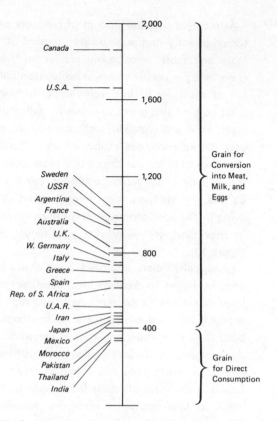

figure 13. *Grain-requirements ladder (pounds of grain used per person per year). Includes grain used for food, feed, seed, and industrial purposes. (From speech given at the Conference on Alternatives for Balancing Future World Food Production and Needs, sponsored by Iowa State University, Center for Agricultural and Economic Adjustment, Ames, Iowa, November 8, 1966.)*

agricultural resources in the industrial countries that are already consuming large quantities of livestock products would be greatly reduced, thereby helping to offset some agricultural stresses on the ecosystem. And in the poor countries, producing enough food to provide adequate diets could be accomplished more quickly and at less cost than would be possible by developing large livestock industries as prerequisites. This means that sufficient nutrition would be attainable in the poor countries without moving as far up the grain-requirements ladder as was essential in the past. These attempts to expand the use of proteins from plants and other sources are highly significant because the production of animal protein cannot be accelerated rapidly enough to meet the world's demands. And even if it could, the strains on the earth's ecosystem would perhaps be unmanageable.

imitation livestock products

Advances in food technology are already beginning to offset some of the increases in grain requirements in the industrial countries by substituting vegetable products for products of animal origin. This change has been most pronounced in the substitution of vegetable oils for animal fats, a substitution made possible on a large scale by the hydrogenation process, which converts vegetable oils (e.g., soybean oil such as Wesson) into solids (such as oleomargarine or Crisco) at room temperature. Oleomargarine is a prime example of a successful livestock-product imitation. In 1940, the average American consumed 14 lb of butter and 2 lb of oleomargarine. In 1970, the figures were 6 lb for butter and 10 lb for oleomargarine. Lard has been replaced almost entirely by hydrogenated vegetable shortenings and is now rarely found in supermarkets in the United States. The low cost of these new products is the major factor in their replacement of authentic livestock products. For example, oleomargarine costs one-quarter to one-half less per pound than butter.

The large-scale substitution of vegetable oils for animal fats has greatly reduced the agricultural resources needed for this category of food. It has also changed the character of dairy and hog production. High fat content in milk has become less desirable, and the preferred hog breeds have shifted from the heavy lard types to the more lean bacon types.

Imitation dairy products other than oleomargarine are also gaining in popularity in the United States. Recent data indicate that an estimated 65 percent of all whipped toppings and 35 percent of all coffee "creams" or whiteners are of nondairy origin, coming from factories rather than dairy farms. Imitation milks, either partly or wholly manufactured, are beginning to make inroads into fluid-milk markets, particularly in the Southwest. The cow is slowly being supplanted by the new processes of converting material of plant origin directly into substitute dairy products. Partly because of this substitution, the number of dairy cows has been reduced, from 26 million in 1940 to 14 million in 1970. The growing substitution for livestock products helps to explain in small part how the American farmer, who was feeding eleven people in 1940, is feeding forty-three in 1970.

Food technologists are now concentrating their efforts on developing acceptable protein substitutes for meat. The first major breakthrough has come with a commercially successful imitation bacon derived largely from soybeans. This product looks and tastes like bacon chips, is high in protein, low in cholesterol, and requires neither cooking nor refrigeration. General Mills is currently building a processing plant in Cedar Rapids, Iowa, to be devoted solely to the production of this bacon substitute. It is an amusing irony that soybeans grown in Iowa will be converted into a bacon substitute through factory processing while on nearby farms corn and soybeans are being turned into bacon through the conventional means.

Replicating the fibrous texture of beef, ham, poultry, and other meats was one of the major obstacles to the development of acceptable substitutes. With the discovery of a technique for spinning vegetable proteins into fibers that can be pressed together, colored, and flavored to simulate the texture of various meats, the way has been opened for the substitution of vegetable for animal protein on a rather massive scale. It is possible that man will be eating plant steaks in the future, plant steaks whose texture, color, consistency, and shape will so much resemble real beefsteak that diners will not know the difference. How rapidly the replacement proceeds will depend, among other things, on the quality of the simulated products and their relative costs. Food technologists can also simulate fish, nuts, and other foods. If these imitations become aesthetically appealing and inexpensive, as well as nutritious, they will have an enormous market potential. Americans are already eating small amounts of flavored, textured soybean "meats" along with real meats in soup mixes, canned stews and chili, frozen ravioli, and frozen hamburger patties.

This technological breakthrough may mean that our great-grandchildren will have to visit the zoo to see cows and pigs. Efficient vegetable substitutes are now available in markets for the entire range of animal fats. The process is just beginning for animal protein: meat, milk, and eggs. Should the substitution of vegetable-derived products for those traditionally coming from livestock continue, it will greatly reduce the land, water, and other resources needed to satisfy food demands.

The manufacture of livestock-product imitations is already spreading from the United States to Europe and Japan, where meat prices are high and low-cost substitutes are therefore appealing. If the technologies are adopted by the poor countries also, some consumers there would be able to move directly from a grain diet to a livestock-substitute diet with foods manufactured locally from indigenous crops.

But developing livestock-product substitutes does not mean that poor countries would not raise livestock at all for widespread domestic consumption. For one thing, there is much land in the world as a whole, and in poor countries in particular, suited for no other agricultural purpose than grazing. Approximately one-fourth of the earth's land area, or 8 billion acres, falls into this category. Raising livestock on such land would not claim agricultural resources necessary for producing cereals or other staples. The great advantage of raising livestock in these circumstances is that they can consume plant materials that otherwise would be unavailable to man as food.

For another thing, poultry, both inherently and especially because of production technologies developed since World War II, are rather efficient converters of grain into animal protein. In fact, it is possible that with expanded grain supplies in some of the developing countries, an explosion will take place in the poultry industry along with developments in food technology, especially in countries where the middle-class urban population is growing.

Furthermore, in recent years a novel way for feeding live-stock has appeared that greatly reduces the resource require-ments for husbanding livestock. American cattlemen are feed-ing urea, commonly used as a nitrogen fertilizer, directly to cattle as a means of reducing the need for adding expensive protein concentrates to feed. Some 300,000 tons of urea were fed to cattle in the United States in 1968, more than is used as fertilizer in many countries. This allows farmers to reduce the protein content of other rations and rely heavily on low-cost roughage, inedible to man, such as corncobs, cornstalks, straw, or sawdust. These roughages are mixed with molasses to make them palatable. Microorganisms in the rumen of the cattle combine the nitrogen and carbohydrates to form protein that the animals can then absorb. Feeding urea to cattle has proved profitable in the United States wherever there is an adequate supply of roughage, as in the corn belt. But an even greater potential for this method exists in the tropics, where low-cost roughage can be produced all year round. It should be much more profitable to feed urea to cattle in Central America, Indonesia, or sub-Saharan Africa than in Indiana or Iowa, where the technique is now widely used.

new protein foods

Food technologists are also evolving another class of high-protein foods that are substitutes for, but not simulations of, livestock products. They are entirely new foods designed to tap vast protein resources (soybean, cottonseed, peanut, and other oilseed meals) that exist in huge quantities but are not ordinarily used as human food.

Widespread protein hunger paradoxically coexists in many poor countries with vast protein resources that are not nor-mally utilized. In India and Nigeria, for example, millions of tons of peanuts are produced for oil to be used in cooking. In other countries, the same is true for coconuts, soybeans, and cottonseed. After the seeds are crushed and the oil extracted, the meal that remains is largely protein. Instead of finding its way directly into the human food supply in these countries, most of the soybean, cottonseed, coconut, and peanut oil meal is fed to livestock, used for organic fertilizer, or exported to earn foreign exchange.

More than 20 million tons of peanut, cottonseed, coconut, and soybean meals are available each year in the poor countries. Making some of this protein into attractive and commercially successful foods would provide a major shortcut to the achievement of protein-adequate diets. There are some serious technical problems: The foods have to be made palatable, and toxic compounds have to be eliminated or prevented from forming. But these obstacles are slowly being overcome, and some successful new foods are starting to appear.

Among these new products are popular beverages based on oilseed meals. Vitasoy, a soya-based beverage produced in Hong Kong, now makes up one-fourth of the soft-drink market there. Saci, currently being produced on a pilot basis by the Coca Cola Company in Brazil, is made of soybeans, caramel flavoring, sugar, and water, all indigenous to Brazil, and is designed to have the nutritional quality of milk. Another soya-based drink, banana-flavored Puma, is now made and marketed in Guyana.

Private food companies are being encouraged to develop high-protein foods using sources of protein indigenous to poor countries. Eleven AID-financed investment surveys are now under way in seven or more developing countries. Powdered-protein mixes for beverages are being developed by Swift in Brazil and by Pillsbury in El Salvador. Other protein beverages and solid foods, nearly all using soya or cottonseed meal, are being designed and test-marketed elsewhere.

An interesting parallel exists between the position of high-protein foods in the poor countries and that of low-calorie foods in the United States several years ago. During the late 1950s, many overweight Americans were seeking ways to reduce caloric intake. New technology, creating the low-calorie food industry, evolved in response to this need. Today a wide range of low-calorie foods is available. The need for more protein in the poor countries may in a similar way create a major new industry as new food technologies evolve.

breeding better foods

The main reason animal products have been so essential to good diets in the past is that plant proteins are of lesser quality than animal proteins. Proteins are composed of amino acids, and the quality of a protein is determined by the composition and balance of the amino acids. Of the approximately twenty amino acids, eight are essential to human nutrition. No single vegetable contains the necessary combination of amino acids required by the human body, whereas meat, fish, milk, and eggs do. When a protein lacks one or more of the essential amino acids, it is ineffectual if eaten alone. Or, when the essential amino acids are present, but in insufficient amounts, the protein does not have maximum value, and more of the protein must be eaten to compensate. It is helpful to think of the essential amino acids in a protein as the staves of a barrel. The value of the protein can rise no higher than the level of the lowest stave.

Corn's protein quality, for example, is limited by deficiencies in lysine and, to a lesser extent, in tryptophan, both amino acids essential for human nutrition. Corn-consuming populations suffer therefore from a shortage of these amino acids in their diet. These deficiencies can be overcome today either genetically, through breeding plant varieties with improved protein content, or biochemically, through fortification of the cereal itself.

Advances in plant breeding provide the most promising and exciting prospects for shortcutting the animal route to high-quality protein. The discovery at Purdue in 1963 of a high-lysine gene in a collection of corn germ plasm opened a new front in man's efforts to combat global protein malnutrition. Scientists at the Rockefeller Agricultural Research Program in Colombia, recognizing the implications of the Purdue discovery for Colombia, where corn is the staple food and where protein malnutrition affects much of the population, obtained a seed sample. From this sample, Rockefeller scientists developed commercial corn varieties with high-lysine content that were released for general use in 1969.

Hogs fed with these high-protein corns on a test basis in

Colombia gained weight twice as fast as those receiving only local corn. Dramatic effects are also being achieved with limited trials on human beings in Colombia. Similarly, encouraging experiments have been carried out in Nigeria with high-lysine corn varieties developed there.

For large corn-eating regions in Latin America and sub-Saharan Africa, high-lysine corn has great attraction. Corn is the staple food in some fourteen countries, accounting for at least half of the food-energy supply in Guatemala, Kenya, Rhodesia, Zambia, and Malawi. If the new high-lysine corn varieties now being released commercially in Colombia, Kenya, Nigeria, and elsewhere replace traditional corn, diets could improve enormously. Where the new corn is used as livestock feed, costly protein supplements would be substantially reduced.

The corn breakthrough has created an awareness of the possibilities of improving cereal protein, triggering research efforts with other grains. This area of research is strategic, since for a major portion of mankind, cereals are the major channel of protein intake. To the extent that high yield and high protein can be incorporated in the same wheat and rice seeds, the prospects for expanding protein supplies are indeed encouraging. Seeds that double yields, as the new wheat and rice varieties do, and raise protein content by one-fourth increase the protein output per acre by 250 percent.

The hunt for a high-yielding, high-protein rice variety analogous to the high-protein corn is going on at the International Rice Research Institute in the Philippines. With a vast collection of rice germ plasm already assembled, improving protein content is primarily a matter of testing, selecting, and breeding. When the right combination is found, it is bound to have a further dramatic impact on nutrition throughout Asia. Looking into the future, it is possible to see the development of man-made cereals of high-protein content, high yield, and high efficiency, such as triticale (see Chapter 10).

fortifying foods

Scientists have developed ways of synthesizing amino acids economically, just as they had earlier synthesized vitamins.

This has made it possible to upgrade the quality of protein in cereals simply by adding the necessary amino acids. Adding 4 pounds of lysine to a ton of wheat, for example, costs only four dollars but results in one-third more usable protein. Adding essential amino acids in correct amounts to plant protein can make it equal in quality to animal protein.

In the larger cities of India, government bakeries are now fortifying wheat flour with lysine, as well as with vitamins and minerals. Bread made with this flour may be the most nutritious marketed anywhere and is referred to as Modern Bread. It is quite literally the staff of life. When fully implemented, this fortification program should result in the marketing of 100 million loaves of highly nutritious bread each year. But perhaps more significantly, it has stimulated private bakeries to fortify their bread as well.

Fortification with synthetic amino acids is not only a short-cut to attaining high-quality protein foods that are alternatives to livestock products; it also has far-reaching potential for producing livestock products more economically. In the United States, lysine is now used in livestock feed, particularly for hogs, where it reduces the protein-meal requirements and feed costs. As in the past in this country, advanced nutritional practices are often used on livestock and poultry long before being used on humans. Japan is forging ahead in the use of lysine and other synthetic amino acids in both livestock feed and human food. Foods fortified with lysine are widely marketed in Japan, and lysine-fortified bread is served in school lunch programs.

In India, several novel ways of increasing lysine intake are being explored. They include using salt and tea as carriers of lysine in much the same way that salt is used as a carrier for iodine in the United States. The fortification of these two commodities, which are widely consumed irrespective of income level, could prove to be a very effective way to upgrade diets.

far-out protein foods

The idea of using algae as food, described by science-fiction writer Jules Verne a century ago, is technically feasible. But little progress has been made toward developing a palatable, commercially usable food product. A source of food from the sea with better prospects of success is fish-protein concentrate. Neutral in taste and color, fish-protein concentrate can be processed from species of fish that are not usually eaten by humans and that are therefore less costly. Because it is tasteless and colorless, it can be added directly to other dishes to boost protein intake, thus avoiding the need to change dietary habits. But, as pointed out in Chapter 7, soy-protein concentrate or peanut meal or lysine additives can do these things, too, and at much less cost with current technologies.

Green leaves of trees offer a somewhat exotic potential source of protein. Leaf protein (about 3 percent) can be extracted and concentrated by a process developed in Britain during the World War II U-boat threat by N. W. Pirie of the Rothamsted Experimental Station. As with some other potential sources of protein, the technical ability exists but the problems of producing leaf protein at competitive costs and introducing it in diets on a scale large enough to be significant remain.

Perhaps the most exotic approach to expanding world protein supplies is the experimental efforts to use petroleum as a feedstock for some of the simplest forms of plant life, such as yeast and other single-cell organisms that are very high in protein (yeast contains 50 percent). With its technical feasibility established, this idea is now being intensively researched by more than a score of multinational petroleum companies. British Petroleum began operating early in 1971 a small plant in France, near Marseilles, that is expected to produce 16,000 tons of protein yearly. The Soviet Union, chronically short of feedstuffs, is reportedly producing single-cell protein of feed quality on a limited scale. Japan is also moving rapidly toward large-scale commercial production.

Promoters of single-cell protein hope it will eventually be fit for humans, but the existing process appears to produce protein suitable only for livestock. Should this technology ever become economically competitive, it would have far-reaching implications for conventional agriculture. And how ironic it is.

164

man and his environment: food

Photosynthesis, occurring eons ago, produced plant material that was eventually converted into petroleum. Now new technology has made it possible for that solar energy to be unlocked and to compete directly with photosynthesis occurring on farms today.

SUGGESTED READINGS

Altschul, Aaron, "Combating Malnutrition: New Strategies Through Food Science," paper presented at the 2nd Joint Meeting of the American Institute of Chemical Engineers and the Institutio de Ingenieros Quimicos de Puerto Rico, Tampa, Florida, May 21, 1968.

Altschul, Aaron, "Food: Proteins for Humans," *Chemical and Engineering News*, November 24, 1969.

Altschul, Aaron, "Food Proteins: New Sources from Seeds," *Science*, October 13, 1967.

Altschul, Aaron, "Using Unused Protein Supplies," *IAD Newsletter*, International Agriculture Development Service, U.S. Department of Agriculture, February, 1968.

Altschul, Aaron, *Protein, Its Chemistry and Politics*, New York: Basic Books, 1965.

Pirie, N. W., "Leaf Protein as a Human Food," *Science*, June 24, 1966.

President's Science Advisory Committee, *The World Food Problem*, Report of the Panel on the World Food Supply, vol. 2, Washington, D.C.: U.S. Government Printing Office, 1967.

12
agricultural
pressures
on the
earth's
ecosystem

Since the beginnings of agriculture, man's successive interventions in the ecosystem have enlarged the earth's population-sustaining capacity several hundredfold, from the estimated 5–10 million of the hunting world to more than 3 billion today. This development, rapid as it was from a geologic-time perspective, took place over more than 10,000–12,000 years. Man is now pressing toward his fourth billion, the addition of which will have taken him only 15 years: from 1960 to 1975. Unless population growth is halted, man may have to enlarge food production by two or three times in the next 30 years to accommodate both an anticipated doubling of his numbers and the almost universal desire for better diets.

The net effect of the projected doubling in man's numbers and hoped-for future gains in income, particularly among the world's poor, is mounting agricultural pressure on the ecosystem. The key question then that man must ask and answer is: Will the earth's ecosystem, already showing signs of strain and stress, hold up under such growing pressure?

Man is placing essentially two kinds of agricultural pressure on the ecosystem in his quest for more food. One may be called *extensive* pressure, since it results from extending cultivation to marginal land. The other is *intensive* pressure because it results from intensifying farming on the existing cultivated area through the increased use of agricultural chemicals, water, and more productive seeds.

With most of the world's readily arable land already being farmed, further expansion of the cultivated area involves bringing increasingly marginal land under the plow, especially in the poor countries. The cost of extending cultivation into such areas is often the loss or destruction of that thin mantle of topsoil on which man depends for his food supply.

Man's increasing numbers invariably result in the cutting of trees on more and more land, either to make room for crops or to meet rising fuel demands. In the more densely populated poor countries, fuel needs have long since exceeded the replacement capacity of local forests. As a result, the forested area has declined to the point where in many parts of the world there is little forest left. Where this is the case, as in the Indo-Pakistan subcontinent or mainland China, people are reduced to using some other source of fuel (such as cow dung) for cooking and heating purposes. Today the number of people in the world who rely on cow dung for fuel probably far exceeds those using some of the more modern fuels such as natural gas or oil.

Increase in human population in the poor countries is almost always accompanied by a nearly commensurate increase in livestock population. As numbers of animals grow so that the supply of draft power, food, and fuel will be expanded, they denude the countryside of its natural grass cover and sometimes contribute to deforestation as well. Professor Robert Brooks of Williams College, formerly a resident in India for several years, provides a graphic example of this situation:

*A classic illustration of large-scale destruction
is afforded by the spectacle of wind erosion in
Rajasthan. Overgrazing by goats destroys the
desert plants which might otherwise hold the soil
in place. Goatherds equipped with sickles attached*

*to 20-foot poles strip the leaves off trees to
float downward into the waiting mouths of famished
goats and sheep. The trees die and the soil
blows away two hundred miles to New Delhi where
it comes to rest in the lungs of its inhabitants and on the shiny cars of foreign
diplomats.* *

Not only goats and sheep but cattle and wild animals as well
contribute to denudation. With each passing year, competition
for remaining forage space becomes more acute. Cattle are
overrunning wildlife refuges in India, consuming the forage
relied upon by deer and antelope. This is threatening the existence of the herbivorous deer and antelope as well as the carnivorous tiger and lion. The same sequence is under way in
much of Africa. Archaeological evidence in Afghanistan indicates that land once supporting large human and animal populations is now abandoned mainly because of overgrazing and
denudation.

Overgrazing by animals, together with progressive deforestation occurring as a result of the human population expansion
of the last few decades, is climaxing in a total denudation of
the countryside in many areas of the poor countries, creating
conditions for a rapid spread of soil erosion by wind and
water. With the press of population, hillsides as well as valleys
and flatlands are bared. As the natural cover that normally
holds soil and retards water runoff is reduced, flood and
drought become more severe.

Someone once defined soil as rocks on the way to the sea.
Over most of the earth's surface, the life-sustaining layer of
topsoil is measured in inches. It takes centuries, sometimes
millennia, to create an inch of topsoil by weathering of rocks.
But in some areas of the world man is managing to destroy this
layer in only a fraction of the time. Natural forces such as
wind, rain, and river floods gradually move soil toward the
ocean. When man removes portions of the earth's vegetation

*Robert R. Brooks, "People Versus Food," *Saturday Review*, September 5, 1970, p. 10.

cover, this movement begins to accelerate, sometimes disas-
trously, thinning the topsoil layer to the point where it will no
longer support agriculture, driving rural population into the cities (as is now happening in Rajasthan, in western India, where
tens of thousands of acres are being abandoned yearly). Literally millions of acres of cropland in Asia, North Africa, the
Middle East, and Central America are being abandoned each
year because severe soil erosion by both wind and water has
rendered them unproductive or at least incapable of sustaining
the local inhabitants using existing technologies.

Not only is topsoil lost and land abandoned because of soil
erosion, but irrigation systems are impaired. Much of the topsoil finds its way into streams, rivers, irrigation canals, and
eventually into irrigation reservoirs. The excessive cutting of
forests in Java, an island of 70 million inhabitants, is causing
silting of the irrigation canals and is steadily reducing the
capacity of existing irrigation systems. Each year the damage
from floods, droughts, and erosion becomes more severe.

West Pakistan provides a dramatic and unfortunate example
of the indirect cost of soil erosion. The recently constructed
Mangla Reservoir, situated in the foothills of the Himalayas and
part of the Indus River system, cost $600 million to construct.
The feasibility studies undertaken in the late 1950s, justifying
investment in this irrigation reservoir, were based on a life
expectancy of at least 100 years. As the rapid population
growth in the watershed feeding the Mangla Reservoir has
progressed, so has the rate of denuding and soil erosion. As a
consequence, the Mangla Reservoir is expected to be completely filled with silt within fifty years or less. Gullies cutting
through the fertile countryside within a half-hour's drive of
Rawalpindi are so deep that they have become minor tourist
attractions reminiscent of America's Grand Canyon and Bad-
lands. West Pakistan could have learned from the history of
ancient Indus valley civilization when the same process of
denudation, flooding, and silting undermined the great cities
of Harappa and Mohenjo-Daro.

History provides us with many examples of man's abuse of
the soil that sustains him. North Africa, once the fertile and

highly productive granary of the Roman Empire, has today lost the natural fertility it once had and is heavily dependent on food imports under the U.S. food-aid program. The barren countryside in Greece and in large areas of Spain, China, South Korea, and Central and South America were once covered with forests and grasslands. Mexico today faces a water crisis rooted in the deforestation of that country by the Spanish during the sixteenth century. Deforestation in northeastern Brazil has contributed heavily to the terrible droughts and hunger famous in that region.

Japan was heading for a severe ecological crisis after World War II because of a program of forest clearing in an effort to gain more land. When it became apparent that deforestation was resulting in massive soil erosion and changes in groundwater level, further clearing was canceled and older forest-protection laws reactivated, thus stabilizing the ecosystem. Japan could afford the inputs necessary to intensify agriculture and to import food.

The United States has also learned about the costs of abusing its rich agricultural inheritance. As a result of overplowing and overgrazing of the southern Great Plains during the early decades of this century, wind erosion gradually worsened, culminating in the dust-bowl era of the 1930s. Dust-laden air masses moving eastward until they blotted out the sun over Washington jolted an alarmed Congress into action that led to the creation of the Soil Conservation Service.

Since the 1930s the United States has learned how to deal rather effectively with soil erosion. Fallowing some 20 million acres a year to accumulate moisture in the soil, constructing literally thousands of miles of windbreaks by planting rows of trees across the Great Plains, and practicing strip farming by alternating strips of wheat with strips of fallowed land to reduce blowing of soil while land was idle put an end to the dust-bowl era. Fortunately, the United States had the slack in its agricultural system to permit large acreages of land to be fallowed. Had the United States not been able to respond in this fashion, much of the southern Great Plains, like the once-fertile valleys of North Africa, would have been abandoned.

The Soviet Union, not benefiting from the U.S. experience, repeated this error by bringing 100 million acres of virgin soil under the plow for wheat cultivation in the early 1960s, only to discover that the region's rainfall was too scanty to sustain continuous cultivation. This project is now referred to as the *virgin lands fiasco*. Once reserve moisture in the soil was depleted, the soil began to blow.

Many of the world's densely populated regions, such as western India, Pakistan, Java, Central America, and China, which face similar problems of severe wind and water erosion of their soils because of acute pressure of human and livestock population on the land, cannot afford to fallow large areas. Their food needs are too pressing. Furthermore, preserving their soil requires a massive effort involving reforestation of hundreds of millions of acres, the controlled grazing of cattle, terracing, contour farming, and systematic management of watersheds, all of which require an enormous array of financial resources and technical know-how not yet in prospect.

Some, however, are trying to reverse the process of soil erosion. China is currently building another great wall, this time with trees to break the winds that sweep across the land from the western steppes. The roots of China's incredible flooding and soil erosion reach back 3,000 years, when forests were cut to increase agricultural land. Israel, too, is attempting, with considerable success, to reverse millennia of soil abuse through reforesting land and reclaiming desert areas. Individuals and groups both within Israel and throughout the world have financed the planting of trees, often one tree at a time.

The significance of soil erosion by wind in the poorer countries goes far beyond the mere loss of topsoil. The process increases particulate matter in the atmosphere, adding to that introduced by industrial activities in the richer countries. Should it be established that an increasing amount of particulate matter in the earth's atmosphere is altering the climate, richer countries would have further reason to provide massive technical and capital assistance to the poor countries to confront together this common threat of mankind.

The alternative to bringing more land, much of it increasingly marginal, under the plow is to shift to a more intensive use of existing farmland. Intensifying agriculture basically involves the use of more inputs per unit of land, particularly agricultural chemicals that are used to increase soil fertility, control insects and other pests, and eradicate weeds. A great expansion in the use of fertilizers and pesticides in the twentieth century has enormously benefited mankind. But it has brought another set of ecological problems, those of environmental pollution, that are concentrated thus far in the rich countries but that threaten to spread in the poor countries as agriculture modernizes and intensifies.

As frontiers have disappeared, man has substituted capital, particularly chemical fertilizers, for the additional land needed but not available. Man's use of chemical fertilizers has risen rapidly over the past three decades. The use of all three principal nutrients—nitrogen, phosphorous, and potassium (potash)—increased seven-fold during the three-decade span from 1940 to 1970. Farmers of the world are adding 40 million tons of nitrogen fertilizer alone to the environment yearly.

Each year the share of man's total food supply attributable to chemical fertilizers increases. As of 1971, it was probably not unreasonable to assume that one-fourth of the world's food supply could be accounted for in this way. If the projected increase in the demand for food resulting from human population and income growth materializes, the use of chemical fertilizers may have to triple between now and the end of the century, since the predominant share of future increases in food production must come from intensified use of land already under cultivation. World fertilizer consumption is now increasing by 10 percent per year.

Even at existing levels of agricultural usage, there are signs of stress on the earth's ecosystem. Runoff of chemical fertilizers from farmlands into rivers, lakes, and underground waters, where they accumulate, is creating serious problems. One is the extensive and well-known phenomenon of *eutrophication*, or overfertilization, of freshwater bodies. Eutrophication can occur over geologic time through natural processes, but in recent history, it has been greatly accelerated by man's activities.

Any organic nitrates and phosphates introduced into fresh water serve as rich nutrients for algae and other aquatic plant life. Algae, particularly, thrive and multiply rapidly. This excessive growth of algae depletes the oxygen supply in lakes, streams, and rivers and thus kills off fish life, beginning with species having high oxygen requirements. Bacterial action on algae masses (and decaying fish) produces foul odors and tastes. Unarrested eutrophication eventually brings about the death of a lake or pond as a body of fresh water, transforming it into a swamp instead.

Animal wastes, particularly from feedlots devoted to factory-style production of livestock and poultry, are also a growing danger to natural water systems. The overall U.S. annual production of livestock wastes has been estimated at more than 1.5 billion tons, or twenty times that of the human population. Most of this waste is disposed of by spreading on land, which allows the nitrates to run off into local water supplies. But this is better than discharging animal waste into rivers.

Agriculture is not the only source of excessive nutrients in water systems. Phosphates, coming largely from detergents, are introduced into rivers from sewers carrying municipal and industrial wastes. And nitrates are a by-product of the internal-combustion engine. In New Jersey, heavily traveled by the automobile, the amount of nitrogen added to the state's soil each year by rainfall picking up and depositing nitrous oxide products of gasoline combustion is sufficiently great that it has to be taken into account in fertilizer recommendations and applications. Some of the nitrate runs into the lakes and rivers (such as the Delaware, Hudson, and Raritan) in New Jersey and adjoining states.

The respective importance of the various sources of inorganic nutrients causing eutrophication is not known. Until recently, for example, fertilizer runoff was largely blamed for the rapidly progressing eutrophication of Lake Mendota in Madison, Wisconsin. Now many scientists think that nitrogen from the exhaust of automobiles and engine-powered boats may be the major source.

The already extensive eutrophication problem has profound

173

agricultural pressures on the earth's ecosystem

implications for the earth's ecosystem, and some way must be found to deal with it. Even in the short run, it can have damaging effects on the supply of potable water, the cycles of aquatic life, and ultimately man's food supply. Lake Erie is a classic model of a lake overcome by advanced eutrophication as a result of man's activities. It may be beyond saving. Lake Baikal in the Soviet Union is another, a magnificent, huge lake that once contained the world's purest water and more than 1,000 unique species of plant and animal life.

Canada has begun to limit the use of phosphates. One local government, in Suffolk County, New York, has banned their use outright. Poultry farmers in Indiana have begun to recycle poultry wastes, actually converting them into new feed for their chickens. These efforts, although giving hope, will have to be joined by others on a large scale if eutrophication is to be halted.

The growing use of chemical fertilizers is causing another, more localized, but hazardous problem: the chemical pollution of drinking water. Nitrates are the main worry, since they, unlike phosphates, leach through the soil to underground water. The nitrate content of well water in certain areas of California and Illinois has risen to toxic levels. Both children and livestock have become ill and sometimes died from drinking water containing nitrates. Excessive nitrate can cause methemoglobinemia, a physiological disorder affecting the blood's oxygen-carrying capacity. Since the problem of increasing nitrates in groundwater is thus far of local dimensions, it can be effectively countered by finding alternative (although usually more costly) sources of drinking water. Bottled water is being used in some California communities.

Man's use of chemical pesticides to protect crops from disease, weeds, insects, and other pests has also become widespread in the twentieth century, contributing greatly to intensified food production. But it, too, is seriously polluting the environment. Usage has risen prodigiously since World War II, when synthetic organic pesticides, such as DDT, that are more potent and cheaper to manufacture than older, simpler organic pesticides became available. Pesticide production in the United

States was 1.16 billion pounds in 1968, up 35 percent from 1965. About one-third of this was exported, and the rest was used domestically. Eighty percent of total production consisted of synthetic organic chemicals. Older pesticides such as arsenic, and lead, mercury, and copper compounds have been used by man for the better part of a century. But with the introduction and spread of synthetic pesticides in the environment in the past twenty-five years or so, particularly the chlorinated hydrocarbons (of which DDT is one), numerous and far-reaching problems have begun to appear.

Pesticides are, of course, poisonous and can be debilitating or lethal to humans and a myriad of species if taken in sufficient dosage. Most major pesticides have fatally poisoned humans at one time or another due to misusage. What sets DDT and other chlorinated hydrocarbons apart from most pesticides is their persistence or durability. They do not break down or decompose readily in nature. DDT, for example, is estimated to have a lifetime of ten years. Thus, while usage on the planet continues, the amount in the environment keeps building. They are also highly toxic and capable of affecting a broad range of life other than the target pest. And they are highly mobile, circulating widely in water and air currents.

The long-term consequences of accumulating nondegradable pesticides such as DDT and some of its even more potent relatives such as dieldrin in the biosphere are not known. It is clear, however, that the use of DDT and other chlorinated hydrocarbons as pesticides and herbicides is beginning to threaten many species of animal life, including man. DDT is today found in the tissues of animals over a global range of life forms from penguins in Antarctica to children in the villages of Thailand, and it is present in your tissues and mine. DDT, although not soluble in water, is soluble in fats and tends to concentrate in animal tissue, particularly fatty organs. The reproductive capacity of some of the predatory birds and fishes is being destroyed at relatively low environmental concentrations of chlorinated hydrocarbons. There is growing evidence that DDT is actually on its way to causing extinction of some species, notably predatory birds such as the bald eagle

175

and peregrine falcon, whose capacity for using calcium is so impaired by DDT that the shells of their eggs are too thin to avoid breakage in the nest before the fledglings hatch. Carnivores are particularly likely to concentrate DDT in their tissues because they feed on herbivores that have already concentrated it from large quantities of vegetation consumed.

Man is perhaps more likely to accumulate high concentrations of DDT in his tissues than many species because he is an omnivore. The average American, for example, consumes more than 100 pounds of beef each year from animals that are, by virtue of their grazing capacity, concentrators of DDT. In the United States, concentrations of DDT in mother's milk now exceed the tolerance levels established for foodstuffs by the Food and Drug Administration. The pressing question here is: What are the long-term effects of rising pesticide concentrations in the environment on human health and well-being?

It is ironic that a Swiss scientist, Paul Hermann Müller, was awarded the Nobel Prize in 1948 for developing DDT, and that less than a generation later, its use is being banned in a number of countries. This illustrates how little is known about the consequences of some of man's interventions in the biosphere. It is unfortunate that the adverse effects of DDT on certain species, particularly the predatory birds, are such that some may become extinct before the growing accumulation of DDT in the environment can be arrested.

DDT is used not only for agricultural purposes but also for killing the malaria-carrying anopheles mosquito that has plagued tropical–subtropical regions in the past. It is also used against other insect-transmitted diseases such as plague, dengue, and sleeping sickness.

Many governments in the wealthier countries are banning the use of DDT because of the desire to preserve valued endangered species and because of concern about the potential effects on man. At the same time, any serious consideration of banning the use of DDT has been barred in the FAO by a membership dominated by poor countries whose concern is not preserving the bald eagle but feeding increasing numbers of people and eradicating malaria. The DDT case provides a good example of how conflicts between the quantity and quality of life will come into focus as pressures on the earth's agricultural ecosystem intensify.

As labor becomes more costly, farmers turn to the use of chemical herbicides to control weeds, with far-flung consequences for the ecosystem. Many of the herbicides used in agriculture are the same kinds used to defoliate areas of Vietnam: 2,4-D; 2,4,5-T. Many of these affect plant life and subsequently animal life in the ocean by contaminating and possibly disrupting food chains. There is some evidence that the single-cell life in the Gulf of Mexico may be affected by 2,4-D coming down the Mississippi River out of the corn and cotton fields.

Several alternative approaches to the problem of controlling pests are being explored. Among the possible substitutes for broad-spectrum, long-lasting poisons such as the chlorinated hydrocarbons are chemical pesticides that are specific to particular insects, diseases, and weeds without affecting other organisms. In addition, scientists are searching for pesticides that will be relatively nontoxic and decompose rapidly in nature after being deposited on vegetation or in the soil. Softer pesticides are, however, more costly.

Researchers are also developing a number of biological controls. Biological control is only in its infancy but is quite promising, and some methods have already been effective. Among the more successful is the sterile male technique, which involves sterilizing large numbers of males of a given insect species. This technique was developed in the United States under the direction of Edward Knipling, now director of entomology research for USDA Agricultural Research Service. The first large-scale use of this technique was on the screwworm fly, a pest of cattle. A large number of male screwworm flies were sterilized by irradiation and then released. These bred with local females that laid infertile eggs. When a high ratio of sterile males is maintained, the population of the screwworm fly decreases. Within the United States, the population of this pest, which costs livestock producers millions of dollars yearly, has been held to negligible levels by releasing 125 million sterile flies weekly wherever the flies reappear, including particularly a 300-mile zone along the Mexican border. The USDA and the Mexican government are now considering pushing the control zone southward to the Isthmus of Panama in order to virtually eradicate the screwworm fly from North America. The cost of this control program is estimated at one-fifteenth of the cost of the annual losses that would be attributable to the screwworm fly in the absence of control. Efforts are now under way to control the Mexican fruit fly and the pink cotton bollworm in California by using this technique.

Breeding pest-resistant plants is another biological control that is meeting with success. At least twenty-two varieties of wheat have been bred that are resistant to the Hessian fly pest. In areas where resistant strains of wheat have been used, the Hessian fly population has been reduced to the point where the pest is no longer a problem. Resistance to the corn borer and corn earworm has been bred into strains of corn. And work is progressing on alfalfa varieties that resist leaf hoppers and aphids.

Still another alternative is the development and planned introduction of insect parasites, ranging from wasplike creatures that lay their eggs in certain other pest insects to bacteria and viruses. Although this method already has a considerable history, there have been few successes to date. When the technique is used in combination with pest-resistant plants, control is more effective.

Rachel Carson warned in the early 1960s about the consequences of accumulating synthetic pesticides in the environment. Since then, some areas have literally had a silent spring. One is the Cañete valley of Peru, where the problems emerging as a result of relying solely on chemical pesticides to control the insect pests of cotton were more serious than those for which they were the antidotes.

Cotton in the Cañete Valley had been attacked by a number of pests: species of leaf worm, bud weevil, cotton aphid, minor bollworm, white scale, and cotton stainer. Before 1939, these pests were controlled by natural predators and parasites, by collecting the insects by hand, and by using older pesticides: nicotine sulfate and arsenic compounds. In 1939, synthetic pesticides were introduced. By 1949, strains of insecticide-resistant target pests had developed. In addition, species that previously were of minor importance had become major pests. Disastrous crop failures ensued. New and stronger pesticides (dieldrin, endrin, and parathion) were eventually applied; they initially gave good control and then declined in effectiveness. The situation became increasingly serious and climaxed in 1956 with a major crop failure. Only with the banning of synthetic organic pesticides in the valley and a return to biological controls, through the introduction of natural predators, and cultural practices was the situation reversed. Cotton yields returned to high levels by 1958.

In the United States, agricultural policies that divert land from production in order to avoid overproduction are unintentionally aggravating the environmental crisis by encouraging the more intensive use of agricultural chemicals. If farm policies were being formulated by ecologists rather than by economists and politicians, as has always been the case, they would be quite different. Rather than diverting land from use to balance supply and demand, an ecologist would probably permit farmers to crop as much land as they wished as long as it did not result in erosion. A tax would then be placed on fertilizer, at least nitrate fertilizer, and harmful pesticides. The tax on these items would be raised and lowered as needed to balance supply and demand. As at present, the net effect of such an approach would be an adequate supply of food, but adverse effects on the environment would be minimized.

Greater knowledge of the effects on all forms of human metabolism of various agricultural chemicals, now so widely used, is sorely needed. And with almost equal urgency, there is need to know how the many other animal and plant species making up the biosphere's complex web of life are being and will be affected. The most worrisome thing is not what man

agricultural pressures on the earth's ecosystem

knows, but what he does not know. Man, in a sense, is using the biosphere as an experimental laboratory with himself among the guinea pigs.

summary

As the demand for food increases in the future as a result of both population growth and rising incomes, particularly among that two-thirds of mankind now poor and malnourished, man will be forced to intervene more and more in the environment while just beginning to understand the consequences of doing so. The use of chemical fertilizers is projected to grow steadily over the remaining decades of this century. The desirability of increased biological control notwithstanding, the use of pesticides to protect crops must also increase greatly as crop stands become more specialized and more lush and as year-round cropping spreads in the tropics. The demand for water for agricultural purposes will most likely far exceed the water available from conventional sources. Man will then be forced to desalt seawater for irrigation purposes or, what may prove more feasible, to alter the world's climatic patterns in order to shift some of the rainfall now located over the oceans to some of the earth's land masses. But the consequences of extending man's intervention to climate control are not known.

Essentially, altering climate requires two technological capabilities. The first is an enormous capacity for gathering information on temperatures, humidity, air-mass movements, precipitation, ocean currents, and many other factors. Enough data must be collected to permit construction of a model of the earth's climatic system. Once this is in hand, a computational facility capable of simulating the system, indicating the effect of man-induced changes in climate, is required. Earth-orbiting satellites provide the information-gathering capacity, and the latest generation of computers supplies the computational capability. As is often the case, technology is far ahead of institutions needed to effectively use it. Until a supranational institution is created to analyze, coordinate, and regulate activities in this field, individual countries and firms should exercise restraint in various activities designed specifically to alter climate, particularly those involving rainfall patterns.

What is clearly needed today is a cooperative effort and, more specifically, a world environmental agency to monitor, research, and regulate man's interventions in the environment, including those made in his quest for more food. Many of his efforts to expand the food supply are global in impact and can only be dealt with in the context of a global institution. The health of the earth's ecosystem can no longer be separated from the global mode of political organization.

SUGGESTED READINGS

Brooks, Robert R., "People Versus Food," *Saturday Review*, September 5, 1970.

Carson, Rachel, *Silent Spring*, Boston: Houghton Mifflin, 1962.

Destler, I. M., "Ecological Imbalance—Man's Pressure on the Land," *IAD Newsletter*, International Agriculture Development Service, U.S. Department of Agriculture, February, 1968.

Fletcher, J. O., "Controlling the Planet's Climate," in *Impact of Science on Society*, vol. 19, no. 2, Paris: UNESCO, April–June, 1969.

Holcomb, Robert W., "Insect Control: Alternatives to the Use of Conventional Pesticides," *Science*, April 24, 1970.

Irving, George W., Jr., "Agricultural Pest Control and the Environment," *Science*, June 19, 1970.

Report of the Secretary's Commission of Pesticides and Their Relationship to Environmental Health, Washington, D.C.: U.S. Government Printing Office, 1969.

Rudd, Robert L., *Pesticides in the Living Landscape*, Madison: University of Wisconsin Press, 1964.

Smith, Ray F., "Integrated Control of Insects," *Agricultural Science Review*, First Quarter, 1969.

Thomas, William L., Jr., ed., *Man's Role in Changing the Face of the Earth*, Chicago: University of Chicago Press, 1956.

"The Water Environment" in *Cleaning Our Environment: The*

agricultural pressures on the earth's ecosystem

Chemical Basis for Action, Washington: American Chemical Society, 1969.

Wurster, Charles F., Jr., "Chlorinated Hydrocarbon Insecticides and the World Ecosystem," *Biological Conservation*, England: Elsevier Publishing Company Ltd, 1969.

13
difficult
choices
ahead

Man today is faced with uncommonly difficult choices. The environmental consequences of his burgeoning quest for food have real costs in terms of the quality of life on the planet and ultimately in terms of the persistence of human life itself. And the costs are mounting.

Agriculture brought a continuing increase in the earth's food-producing and population-sustaining capacity. Agriculture also brought man a capacity for intervening in the environment unmatched in any other area of human activity. Agricultural man's early attempts to shape his environment to his needs were simple, but over time, they have become much more complex. Initial interventions affected only local areas, but those of modern agriculture often have global consequences and incalculable costs.

eutrophication

The costs of increasing the food supply are many. Among the major ones already evident is the loss of freshwater bodies due to eutrophication. Man's quest for food is converting literally hundreds, probably thousands, of freshwater lakes and streams into algae-laden swamps throughout North America, Europe, and now increasingly in those poor countries where fertilizer usage is beginning to climb. The costs of rescuing or reclaiming dying or eutrophic lakes is enormous. Lake Erie, the best-known victim, has received nutrients from both agricultural and industrial sources. An estimated $50 billion, the equivalent of the Department of Interior budget for the next twenty-two years at the current level, would be required to restore Lake Erie to its original state as a freshwater body. Sweden recently paid $10 million to reclaim a very small lake.

No one has calculated the cost to mankind of losing these freshwater lakes and streams, but it must be staggering. No one is even maintaining an inventory of lakes threatened by eutrophication. Eutrophication is reducing the fish catch from freshwater lakes and streams and even from parts of the ocean. New rice strains are dramatically boosting rice output in the Philippines and elsewhere in Asia, but the fertilizer needed to realize their genetic potential is causing the eutrophication of lakes and streams, depriving villages of fish that were once an important part of their diet. In effect, the modernization of agriculture is expanding the food supply but forcing man to sacrifice some of the fish-protein supply in the process. Not only is man deprived of the protein from fish once harvested from these lakes, but he is also losing recreational facilities. In 1970, the U.S. government conducted the first survey of lake and ocean beaches in the United States. Ninety-one beaches were found unfit for human use. Eutrophication from agricultural nutrients has caused some of this loss—no one knows how much.

Possibilities for dealing with the eutrophication threat posed by steadily expanding use of fertilizer are not plentiful, given the lack of viable alternatives to fertilizer. Assuming an effort is made to double food production, how many of the world's freshwater lakes will have become eutrophic ten years hence, or by the end of the century? Or perhaps more appropriately, how many freshwater lakes will remain fresh if we move toward a situation where the world's farmers are spreading, say,

200 million tons, in contrast with the current 70 million tons, of chemical fertilizers on their land each year in an effort to produce the needed food?

endangered and
lost species

Another major area of cost to man and to the planet's complex of life resulting from enlarging agricultural intervention into the environment is the endangering and loss of species. Agriculture is threatening the existence of species by destroying habitats and by introducing toxic materials into the environment. No one knows exactly how many species of birds, fish, and mammals, let alone plants, are threatened by man's agricultural efforts. Wild elephants in Ceylon now number no more than 2,500, less than half the elephant population of twenty years ago. Their sources of subsistence are diminishing steadily as their forest and jungle habitat is cleared to produce food for the island's human population, now doubling every twenty-three years. The Bengal tiger is also endangered.

Almost everyone knows that the peregrine falcon, the world's fastest bird, and the bald eagle, the U.S. emblem, are endangered by pesticides. If the bald eagle becomes extinct, as some naturalists expect, would the United States retain the eagle as the national emblem, basing future designs on historical records, or would it turn to some living species? Would Benjamin Franklin's suggestion, reproposed recently by Britain's Princess Anne, be taken that the turkey, the only domesticated fowl indigenous to the United States, become the emblem?

What is not well known is that many other birds are threatened by pesticides. Louisiana's state bird, the brown pelican, has disappeared from that state and is decreasing in California and Florida because of pesticide-induced thin-shelled eggs. In Utah, the population of the white-faced ibis crashed in one year from 5,200 to 900 birds because of thin eggshells. In Denmark, the return of the storks from wintering in North Africa has long been a national event, celebrated by young and old alike. At one time, 10,000 storks arrived each year. Last year, only 70 pairs came. Pesticides used to protect crops from the locust threat in the Nile valley are believed to be largely responsible.

Pravda reports the reckless use of chemical pesticides in agriculture is decimating many forms of wildlife in the Soviet Union, causing many species to become zoological rarities. The duck-hunting season was canceled entirely in 1970 because of the diminishing flocks of wild ducks. The *New York Times* quotes *Pravda:* "This question [the extinction of species] is worrying us more and more every year. Why do we see almost no flocks of geese and cranes in April? Almost all the partridges are gone. Our woods, gardens and fields are becoming quieter and quieter." Is Rachel Carson's prediction of a sterile countryside coming true?

Thus far during this century, an average of one species per year quietly made its exit somewhere in the world. As the number of human beings goes up, the number of extant species is going down. The Department of the Interior now maintains a list of endangered species within the United States, totaling seventy-nine in early 1970. By October, 1970, three mammals, eight birds, and eleven types of fish were added to the list. One worldwide list of endangered species, although obviously far from complete, now includes 275 mammals and 300 species of birds threatened with extinction. No one knows how many species of fish are threatened.

What is the rule of thumb for converting the current annual global increase in human population of 73 million into extinct species of mamals, birds, and fish? Does such an increase cost an average of three species per year? Or ten? What will the situation be 10 years hence if we continue on our present course? And further, how does man grasp the meaning of the loss of any one, or of many, species? Man holds the future of the planet's life in his trust. If his intrusion into the environment has proceeded to the point of causing the extinction of increasing numbers of species, it has proceeded too far, for moral reasons and perhaps for his own security. Perhaps it is time to adopt a bill of rights for the earth's wildlife.

Unfortunately, a large number of the species threatened may

already be doomed to extinction, either because the numbers are already too small to perpetuate the species or because the conditions threatening their survival, such as the levels of DDT now circulating in the biosphere, cannot be altered. The sad thing is that the process is irreversible. A species that becomes extinct is lost not only to us but to our children and to theirs for all time to come. Beyond this, we have little understanding of the effect on the web of life of the loss of a large number of species.

modification of climate

Modification of climate is a third major area of trouble resulting from man's perennial quest for more food. Agriculture is contributing greatly to the creation of dust bowls in many places, particularly in the poor countries. The result, as pointed out in Chapter 12, is a rise in the particulate matter in the atmosphere. Some scientists feel that this increase in particulate matter, which may be reducing the amount of solar energy reaching the earth, is partly responsible for the decline in average temperature at the earth's surface of nearly one-half degree Fahrenheit over the past twenty-five years. Dr. Gordon MacDonald, a member of the President's Council on Environmental Quality, points to an associated southward shift in the frost boundaries and heavy ice in the North Atlantic hindering the activities of Icelandic fisherman. He further points out that a cooling trend of only a few degrees in the earth's fragile and delicately balanced climatic system could initiate another Ice Age. University of Wisconsin meteorologist Reid A. Bryson points out that a shift in weather patterns in recent years in Wisconsin has resulted in somewhat warmer, snowier winters and colder summers. Such climatic changes carried to an extreme could produce snowfalls which do not completely melt away during summer months, seriously affecting agricultural and recreational industries. Thus we must reckon with the prospect that man's effort to expand his food supply may be altering the earth's climate in a way that will affect the complex of human activity, the existence of species, and the quality of life.

The possible affecting of the earth's climate by increasing atmospheric particulate matter has thus far been an unintended consequence of man's quest for food. But man is now planning interventions that he knows full well will have the side effect of climate alteration. The Soviet plan to turn around four rivers now emptying into the Arctic Ocean, diverting them southward, will increase irrigation water required for greater food output. But shutting off this flow of warm water into the Arctic will undoubtedly alter the climate there, and this, in turn, will affect the global climatic pattern. Again, no one knows exactly how, but the Soviets are proceeding despite protests by meteorologists, arguing that they need the additional food this water will produce.

And further, man is trying to harness atmospheric moisture directly to move rainfall where he wants it even though he cannot yet predict the additional effects of this intentional and direct intervention. There are now firms headquartered in Washington, D.C., that are in the business of rainmaking internationally. They will contract with national or local governments or farmers' associations to produce rain anywhere in the world. Unfortunately, there is no supranational institution to regulate this activity, holding out the prospect that nations may one day use advanced weather-modification technologies to compete with each other for potential rainfall in much the same way armies have traditionally fought for control of land. In the absence of global regulatory institutions, one could readily envisage competition between India and Pakistan to shift the life-giving monsoon northward or southward, depending on the particular country's interests. Thus, the combination of growing pressures to expand the food supply, coupled with the advancing technologies at his disposal, have led man to intervene directly in the functioning of the earth's climatic system itself, risking both adverse ecological and social consequences.

What changes will occur in the earth's climate between now

and the end of the century? If soil-erosion trends continue to accelerate, will the concentration of dust particles in the upper atmosphere continue to reinforce the worldwide cooling trend in evidence since 1940? Will the turning around of Soviet rivers do so? In what other ways will the global climatic system be affected?

population growth

As we weigh the consequences of continuing population growth, we are forced to reassess the threat of uncontrolled human fertility. Ever since Thomas Malthus published his treatise on the *Principle of Population* in 1798, man has defined or perceived the population problem largely in terms of food supplies and the threat of famine. It is time to reformulate the problem. The relevant question in any effort to project the food situation into the future is no longer simply: Can we produce enough food? It is: What are the environmental consequences of attempting to do so?

Looking to the future, it is clear that man's food–population–environment crisis assumes disturbing dimensions. As the costs of continually expanding food production become clearer, they bring into great doubt whether the earth's ecosystem can sustain increasing populations. As pointed out in an earlier chapter, United Nations demographic projections indicate a near doubling of man's numbers by the end of the century. Feeding these numbers, should they materialize, at current dietary levels would require a doubling of current food-production levels. Stated simply, the increase in the earth's food-producing capacity over the next three decades would have to match that developed from the time agriculture was invented until the present.

Doubling food production just to maintain current dietary levels would challenge world agriculture and result in staggering pressures on the earth's ecosystem. But "at current dietary levels" means hundreds of millions of human beings are malnourished. If, at the same time, we take seriously the goal of eliminating hunger and malnutrition by the end of the century and depend on conventional means to do so, we must raise food production far more, perhaps nearly tripling current levels. Would this be achieved by clearing more and more land or by merely intensifying the use of land under cultivation through the use of more chemical fertilizers, pesticides, and water? Even a doubling of food production by the end of the century would require nearly a tripling of fertilizer use, and tripling food production would require even more fertilizer.

Very little has been done to inventory and weigh costs and losses associated with efforts to continually expand the world food supply to meet pressing, ever-increasing food needs. Information is lacking on a global scale, and thinking has been handicapped by this lack of information. Complex questions, such as those stated above, must be asked and answered, and not even the world's wisest men now know the answers. But man has enough information to know that the costs of continually expanding the food-producing capacity of the earth are high and cannot be borne indefinitely. He knows, too, that population growth, fueling the exponential increases in food requirements, lies at the core of the dilemma. Man, pressing more and more against the finite limits of the earth's ecosystem, is forced to face the stark reality that there is a tradeoff between increases in human numbers and improvements in the quality of life.

It should be at least pointed out that rapid population growth, at a time in history when most of the earth's land frontiers have disappeared, is affecting the quality of human life in other critical ways as well. Population growth in rural areas has reached the point where the countryside is unable to continue absorbing people indefinitely in productive employment either within the framework of traditional agriculture or within that of modern agriculture. The world's population remains predominantly rural at present, with more than half of mankind living in rural Asia, Africa, and Latin America. And despite migration away from the coutryside, rural populations are expanding in virtually all poor countries (except Taiwan, Turkey, and Israel) and are projected to do so for years, if not decades, to come.

While the number of young people seeking employment in

the farming regions of the earth is sharply rising because of the explosion of population, new land available for cultivation is declining in many countries. Plots of land divided and subdivided for generations cannot readily accommodate further increases in human numbers. Landholding agreements and economic policies, rather than land scarcity as such, are blocking opportunity in the countryside in other countries, mainly in Latin America and sub-Saharan Africa. And in most rich countries, intensive mechanized agriculture geared to large farms prevents the absorption of increasing numbers in modern agriculture. Millions of people remaining in the countryside in the poor countries are joining an army of seasonally unemployed and landless farm laborers, a situation that exacerbates hunger, rural poverty, and political unrest. In crowded India, the landless rural labor force now exceeds the total population of Great Britain.

Rapid population growth and the lack of opportunity in the countryside are also acting to reshape human settlement patterns by forcing and accelerating the migration of people to cities, creating even more problems for late twentieth-century man. Man's most enduring social phenomenon since the Industrial Revolution has been the steady movement of his numbers from the farm to the city. But the migration from countryside to city projected for the seventies in Asia, Latin America, and Africa will be the largest migration history has witnessed. In the past, the scale of waves of migration from countryside to city, from Europe across the Atlantic to America, and from the east coast of North America westward, did not approach even remotely the rural–urban migration now in prospect.

Cities in the poor countries are not ready for this influx. They are not industrializing, modernizing, or producing jobs fast enough or on a scale large enough to accommodate the newcomers. In the poor countries, rapid urbanization is running ahead of industrialization and significant economic growth, in contrast with nineteenth- and twentieth-century industrial centers of Europe and America that in effect pulled people from the farm to the city. People being pushed out of the countryside today by lack of opportunity are moving into

cities and filling urban slums, forming ghettos of unemploy-
ment, poverty, and desperation, called *bustees* in India, *favel-
las* in Brazil, and *gecekondo* in Turkey.

This massive rural–urban migration is affecting urban ecosystems adversely, making it difficult, if not impossible, to
provide the basic amenities and thereby diminishing the quality
of life. For example, two decades of exploding population
growth in West Bengal, the result of successful malaria-eradica-
tion projects and other medical advances, increased the pressure of man on the land to the point where literally millions of
Bengalis had neither land nor the prospect of enough employment in the countryside to ward off starvation. Desperation
drove them to the city, in this case, Calcutta, which, with
50 percent of its families now living in one room or less (the
"or less" includes at least 100,000 people living on the side-
walks), could become the model city of the future. Not only
do new urban immigrants have insufficient space and housing
and services, but they lack even more rudimentary amenities
such as clean water and air. In Latin America, enlarging urban
settlements that are destroying the landscape and polluting
water systems, such as the La Plata River, with human sewage
are being defined as the region's number-one environmental
problem.

The movement from countryside to city is a universal phenomenon. But the plight of the cities is even worse in the poor
countries than in the rich, where there has been at least some
reverse trek from the inner cities to the suburbs. The density
of the ghettos in big cities like New York is not greater and
may even be somewhat less than it was a generation ago. But
there is no such hope of escape from Calcutta, Bombay, or
Bogotá. In countries like India, where the number of cities is
small relative to population, the urban crisis is particularly
acute. Failure to confront this threat to the cities means that
they may be overwhelmed with people, resulting in a socio-
environmental crisis of unthinkable proportions.

In the light of accumulating information, it becomes clear
that we must harness population growth, stabilizing man's
numbers not at some point in the next century, but within the

next couple of decades. The green revolution, by fending off the threat of imminent famine, has bought time, perhaps fifteen or twenty years, to control human fertility. Time is short and is not being well used. The green revolution has been under way for several years already. But little progress has been made in slowing population growth—or, for that matter, in eradicating malnutrition.

eradication of hunger

Man has won this brief reprieve from the threat of famine at a time when the planet has resources for overcoming malnutrition. For the first time in history, it is realistic for mankind to set the goal of eliminating hunger and malnutrition. Breakthroughs in cereal production and the new food technologies (described in Chapter 11) give man an array of tools never before available.

What is needed is the creation of national strategies, on a country-by-country basis, that would embrace several components. An effective national strategy would take advantage of the new high-yielding, high-protein cereals, disseminating them widely and rapidly. It would also encourage a continuous effort by plant breeders to develop high-yielding, high-protein cereals adaptable to an even broader range of growing conditions and tailored to satisfy consumer preferences. Furthermore, it would embody the new technologies for developing poultry and livestock industries, for manufacturing high-protein foods from vegetable sources, and for fortifying foods with vitamins, minerals, and essential amino acids. It would also attempt to formulate a food-price policy that could both maintain incentive prices for farmers and at the same time lower prices to consumers as soon as declining production costs permit. Shaping a plan to balance and manage the complexities of the green revolution, and to do it quickly, is not easy. The poor countries will need help from the rich countries in fashioning and actualizing such plans.

In today's world, malnutrition is inextricably linked with poverty. Data indicate that average national diets do not generally become nutritionally adequate until per capita incomes approach $400 per year. Even with the given technologies, it is not possible to achieve adequate diets under any circumstances, no matter how optimal the technologies and policies, with national per capita incomes less than $200 per year. Eradicating most of the hunger and malnutrition in the world means that man must raise to adequate levels the incomes of that half of the world's people whose incomes are less than $100 per year. It also means expanding employment and raising purchasing power so that food is distributed evenly enough among the population.

The modern agricultural technologies now being introduced into the poor countries are influencing overall employment through their effect on labor needs in agriculture and through the creation of additional employment in agribusiness. In addition, if the new seeds continue to act as engines of change, facilitating greater overall growth in the economies of the poor countries, this will create further employment.

But the future of the green revolution and its potential for overcoming poverty and hunger will depend more and more on whether exportable surpluses of cereals from the poor countries can enter the rich countries. Introduction of the new seeds into the tropical–subtropical regions, with their greater abundance of solar energy and year-round growing temperatures, is strengthening the competitive position of the poor countries. But just when many of the tropical and subtropical countries are beginning to produce exportable surpluses of cereals, many of the rich industrial countries such as Japan and the members of the European Economic Community are pursuing protectionist policies. These trends are leading to a confrontation between rich and poor countries. If the poor countries cannot gain access to the markets of the rich countries, their overall development will be thwarted.

An even greater distortion exists in world sugar production than in cereals. At present, much of the world's sugar comes from sugar beets. But if economics alone prevailed, there would be little if any beet sugar produced in the world. Sugar would come from cane, and virtually all of it from the tropical and subtropical countries. The production of sugar is one commodity in which the poor man living in the tropics has a pronounced advantage over his counterpart in the temperate regions. Beet sugar costs between six and nine cents a pound to produce, whereas cane sugar costs only two to three cents.

Virtually all the industrialized countries in North America and both Eastern and Western Europe, are guilty of protecting inefficient beet sugar production. If the gap between rich and poor is ever to be narrowed, the barriers to sugar imports in the rich countries must be lowered. The failure to do so will not only frustrate the poor countries, but will also deprive them of one of the few competitive advantages nature has given them.

Because mankind today has the technology and resources to remove hunger from the world, its continued existence is a dramatic illustration of man's inhumanity to man. There are growing indications that the two-thirds of mankind who reside in the planet's great southern ghetto and who are becoming aware of how the other one-third live will not tolerate hunger and severe deprivation for an indefinite period, anymore than Blacks in the ghettos of American cities did in the 1960s.

Given the steadily advancing demand for food, further intervention in the earth's ecosystem for more food is inevitable. Man must strive to preserve the ecosystem while endeavoring to ensure adequate food supplies and diets for all mankind. One way to reduce agricultural pressure is to lower the position of high-income man on the food chain by reducing the amount of animal products consumed. Some consumption trends within the United States are moving in this direction. Both milk and egg consumption have declined more than 20 percent since 1950, as Americans have made the transition to a more sedentary way of life and as food technology has made possible growing substitution of vegetable oil and protein for animal products. Countering these trends, however, is an increase in beef consumption from 55 pounds per person yearly in 1940 to 110 pounds in 1968. On balance, this may have more than offset the reduction in pressure on the ecosystem resulting from the reduction in milk and egg con-

*difficult
choices ahead*

sumption and the substitution of vegetable oils for animal fats. If agricultural pressures on the earth's ecosystem become too severe, we may eventually be forced to substitute beans, such as soybeans, for steak even as we slow population growth.

While striving to reduce the pressure of the growing demand for food, man must also seek to reduce the destructive nature of his agricultural interventions. Substituting biological controls, using more expensive pest-specific and biodegradable pesticides, and breeding pest-resistant crops are among the known ways of reducing the adverse impact of pesticides on the earth's complex of life. Using pelletized fertilizer could reduce at least somewhat the adverse effects of excessive chemical nutrients on the earth's bodies of water and on marine life. If it should be determined that rising levels of particulate matter in the atmosphere from the dust bowls are adversely affecting the earth's climate, the rich countries would find it in their interest to provide massive capital and technical assistance to the poor countries, joining them in confronting this common threat.

The food–population–environmental crisis underlines the common dilemma of man in the late twentieth century wherever he lives. Effectively addressing it means reordering priorities—global, national, personal—attaching much greater importance to stabilizing our numbers than is currently the case.

Stabilizing man's numbers will require an enormous educational effort to inform mankind of the possible consequences of continuing on our current procreative path. It will also require making the means to limit births available to women and men everywhere. Such is intended in the United States with the December 1970 enactment of the Family Planning Service and Population Research Act. This landmark legislation is meant to provide free family-planning information and contraceptives to every woman in the United States who requests them. Adoption of such a system worldwide would make a significant dent in the global birth rate, since a sizable share of the 73 million annual population increase consists of the unwanted births that occur in every society. Safe abortion on demand should become available everywhere, not just in a few countries and states. This would be a start, at least.

Mankind is confronted with an urgent need to shift global priorities, attacking poverty and population growth with resources as well as rhetoric. For contrary to the ideas of cold war leaders from both East and West, population and poverty are the great and growing threats to survival and quality of life on the planet. Fighting yesterday's battles, funneling time, attention, and global resources into preparation for war, may be forfeiting the future. Effectively addressing the food-population–environmental crisis means greatly reducing the $200 billion yearly global military expenditure and shifting these scarce public resources into the attack on poverty and the control of human fertility.

Efforts to stop world population growth and overcome poverty must begin at home. Americans cannot make a credible case for global population stabilization without first having a policy and plans for bringing U.S. population growth to a halt. As more information on the ecological straits in which man now finds himself becomes available, an organization such as the newly established, nationwide Zero Population Growth becomes uncommonly relevant, crucial, and deserving of personal support.

Americans cannot expect the world to shift its priorities unless the United States, controlling close to 40 percent of the world's productive resources, changes its national priorities. A foreign policy budget of $78 billion, 75 billion of which is military and 3 billion of which goes to help developing countries, principally in the form of food aid and loans that must be paid back, is not consistent with the long-term interests either of the United States or of mankind. Moreover, a reordering of personal priorities is called for in the United States. Americans must be willing to convert some of the resources going into greater affluence—second home, family boat, third car—into resources to eliminate poverty in the poor countries. Given the levels of income and productivity prevailing in the industrial world, the magnitude of the global poverty problem is no longer unmanageable. The average annual increase in the

*difficult
choices ahead*
U.S. national income is equal to the total annual income of India's 540 million people.

Eliminating poverty and slowing population must be as important to this generation as rebuilding Europe was to the generation that sponsored the Marshall Plan. The stakes are at least as high. Isolationism in a finite biosphere is unthinkable. The American future is inextricably intertwined with that of the rest of mankind.

index

73 74 75 76 9 8 7 6 5 4 3 2